BLACK FACES *of* WAR

A LEGACY OF HONOR FROM THE AMERICAN REVOLUTION TO TODAY

ROBERT V. MORRIS

Foreword by LT. GEN. JULIUS W. BECTON JR., USA (Ret.)

ZENITH PRESS

For my family.

◆ ◆ ◆

First published in 2011 by Zenith Press, an imprint of MBI Publishing Company,
400 1st Avenue North, Suite 300, Minneapolis, MN 55401 USA.

Unless otherwise noted, all images provided courtesy the Morris Collection, Des Moines, Iowa.

The information in this book is true and complete to the best of our knowledge. All recommendations are made without any guarantee on the part of the author or Publisher, who also disclaim any liability incurred in connection with the use of this data or specific details.

This publication has been prepared solely by MBI Publishing Company and is not approved or licensed by any other entity. We recognize that some words, model names, and designations mentioned herein are the property of the trademark holder. We use them for identification purposes only. This is not an official publication.

Zenith Press titles are also available at discounts in bulk quantity for industrial or sales-promotional use. For details write to Special Sales Manager at MBI Publishing Company, 400 1st Avenue North, Minneapolis, MN 55401 USA.

To find out more about our books, join us online at www.zenithpress.com.

Editor: Steve Gansen
Design Manager: Brenda C. Canales
Cover Designer: John Barnett, 4 Eyes Design
Interior Designer: Erin Fahringer

Front cover images: National Archives, except for the following: top row, second from left, and bottom row, far right: U.S. Army; top row, second from right: Archive Photos/Getty Images; middle row, far left: Ohio Historical Society; and bottom row, second from right: Library of Congress.
Frontispiece: "United We Win," World War II–era poster.
Title page: Staff Sergeant Timerlate Kirven (left) and Cpl. Samuel J. Love Sr., the first African Americans decorated with Purple Hearts by the famed 2nd Marine Division. They received their decorations for wounds received in the Battle of Saipan. *National Archives*

Library of Congress Cataloging-in-Publication Data
Library of Congress Cataloging-in-Publication Data

Morris, Robert V.
  Black faces of war : a legacy of honor from the American Revolution to today / Robert V. Morris.
    p. cm.
  ISBN 978-0-7603-3917-6 (hb w/ jkt)
  1. African American soldiers--History. 2. African American soldiers--Biography. 3. United States--Armed Forces--African Americans--History. 4. United States--History, Military. I. Title.
  E185.63.M67 2011
  355.0089'96073--dc22
                              2010032913
Printed in China

Contents

Foreword

THE PAGES OF HISTORY point out a simple fact—that is, there is no gender, race, or religious requirement to love your country and to serve it as a soldier, marine, sailor, or airman. Warriors come from no class. Heroes have no special color. Men and women of color have served America from the time of the colonies and through America's growth as an independent nation. Transplanted unwillingly, they gave their all to their owners and then to their new nation. Blacks fought for America's freedom, yet waited beyond Abraham Lincoln's famous "four score and seven years" to get their freedom and another hundred years to get an often grudgingly given equal opportunity for jobs. Yet blacks, both men and women, always have shown an unbreakable spirit, love of country, and selfless courage.

I was privileged to serve in three wars: in the Pacific in a segregated division that had to fight prejudice to be able to fight the enemy, initially in an all-black battalion within the white 2nd Division in Korea, and in a "colorless" airborne division in Vietnam. I endured all the problems associated with the civil-rights struggle, yet did so willingly for one reason: I loved my country, and I knew that it would someday change.

Black Faces of War shows you some of these men and women, a tiny number compared to the hundreds of thousands that served proudly since America fought to be free. Their faces and their words are representative of so many that went before, so that those who came after could enjoy the freedom for all men that America had promised.

I know their story well, as I was one of them. They still inspire me to have marched with them, but their faces and their sacrifice remind me that love of country is not just for history. It is for today and for every day that follows. It is certain that these men and women gave us something to live up to, but more importantly, they remind us that every generation owes service to their God, their country, and especially to each other.

I walked with heroes in many fields—the armed forces, education, public service. I thank God for the opportunities and for the fact that I did it of my own free will. We must never stop going forward as the citizens of a free nation— our nation—and never forget those who helped put us on their path.

Remember these men and women. They represent a tiny few from the many. And remember, they were all Americans.

—Lt. Gen. Julius W. Becton Jr., USA (Ret.)

Lieutenant General Becton is a veteran of the Korean War and the Vietnam War and former commanding general of VII Corps in Cold War Europe. He also served as director of FEMA and as superintendent of the Washington, D.C., public school system prior to co-chairing the Military Leadership Diversity Commission, which evaluates and assesses policies that provide opportunities for the promotion and advancement of minority members of the U.S. Armed Forces.

Introduction

I BELIEVE THAT, with the exception of the black church, no institution has had a more profound and progressive impact on black Americans than the military, with its benefits, like the GI Bill, that created the black middle class of today. As the son and grandson of two decorated U.S. Army officers and combat veterans, who also happened to be black, it is my duty and responsibility to tell their story and the stories of others who led the charge for equal rights and opportunity.

The powerful photographs displayed on these pages reveal our pain and suffering, along with our determination to win. The text reveals individual and group stories of courage in the face of combat death and of the strength to endure the depths of racial discrimination and become leaders for change.

Black Faces of War leads you through the ugly institution of slavery and its cunning warriors, like Harriet "Moses" Tubman and Henry "Box" Brown, as well as the slave lore that sustained the spirit of our people. It relates the heroics of Crispus Attucks and Peter Salem in the Revolutionary War and Frederick Douglass's call to arms in the Civil War. The 10th Cavalry Buffalo Soldiers protected settlers on the Western frontier and saved future U.S. President Teddy Roosevelt on San Juan Hill.

James B. Morris describes the first black officer class, which trained at Fort Des Moines, Iowa, in 1917. James Mitchell gives first-person testimony on the 92nd Division in World War I France and the experience of coming home to Georgia in 1919, during the what became known as the Blood Red Summer, and barely escaping the noose.

Luther H. Smith discusses his 133 combat missions as a World War II Tuskegee airman and his experience as prisoner of war (POW), while Virgil Dixon shares the deadly realities of tank warfare with the 758th Tank Battalion in Italy. The first black and female officer in the Women's Army Auxiliary Corps (WAAC), Charity Adams Earley, reveals the often-bitter history of the new female soldiers at Fort Des Moines in 1942, and Arlene Roberts-Morris recounts how, as a civilian black woman, she contributed to the war effort during World War II by working in the office that developed the atomic bomb. Captain James "Braddie" Morris Jr. recalls breaking the color line as a black officer with the 6th Army "Alamo Force" in the South Pacific during World War II.

Black U.S. Army medic George Johnson describes the first real combat integration in the deadly hills of Korea, described by many as America's most difficult war, while young marine Clarence Burnough details his near-fatal visit to Vietnam's scary A Shau Valley. Brigadier General Arnold Gordon-Bray describes the evolution of leadership and today's war on terror.

Black Faces of War is a celebration of the sacrifice and courage of the brave black men and women who have allowed us to succeed in every endeavor of American society, all the way to the White House and beyond.

CHAPTER 1

The American Revolution, Slavery, and the Antebellum South

Death of Crispus Attucks at the Boston Massacre by James Wells Champney (American artist, 1843–1908). *Bridgeman Art Library*

FROM CESAR BROWN and Barzillai Lew to Prince Hall and Cato Tufts, the names of early American black patriots are lost in the maze of history, labeled as escaped slaves and freemen fighting for their future. On 5 March 1770, a lanky runaway slave and seaman named Crispus Attucks led a crowd against the British Army and was shot down in what would become the Boston Massacre.

The cover of a comic book from Fitzgerald Publishing's Golden Legacy Series (1967): "Crispus Attucks and the Minutemen." *Fitzgerald Publishing Company*

Here was a fugitive slave who, with his bare hands, was willing to resist England to the point of giving his life. It was a remarkable thing, the colonists reasoned, to have their fight for freedom waged by one who was not as free as they.

—John Hope Franklin,
From Slavery to Freedom,
about Crispus Attucks

Attucks became the first American to die in the Revolutionary War, but he was far from the last. Nearly fifty years old, Attucks had escaped his enslavement under a Framingham, Massachusetts, master aboard a ship leaving the Boston Harbor more than twenty years earlier. Attucks's tombstone reads:

Long as in Freedom's cause the wise contend,
Dear to your country shall your fame extend;
While to the world the lettered stone shall tell
Where Caldwell, Attucks, Gray and Maverick fell.

Although blacks were already serving as Minutemen and in many local militias fighting Indians, the Continental Congress established integrated Minutemen militias to respond if the British attacked in 1775. Blacks soldiers fought bravely at Lexington, Concord, and the Battle of Bunker Hill, where freeman Peter Salem shot British commander Maj. John Pitcairn after the major demanded that American forces there surrender.

Aaron White wrote a letter to historian George Livermore in 1862 in response to Livermore's inquiry: "Pitcairn's commanding air at first startled the men immediately before him. They neither answered or fired. At this critical moment, a Negro soldier [Salem] stepped forward, and aiming his musket directly at the major's bosom, blew him through." (Katz 1967)

A sketch of the Battle of Bunker Hill (June 1776) shows the slave Peter Salem helping repulse an attack by British forces by shooting their commander, Maj. John Pitcairn. Salem's action earned him his freedom and a military pension.

Slave Salem Poor's Battle of Charlestown heroics became so legendary that a petition requesting his freedom was made to the U.S. Congress in his honor by the white officers serving with him (original spelling, punctuation, and capitalization preserved):

> The subscribers begg leave, to Report to your Honorable House (which we do in justice to the character of so Brave a Man), that, under Our Own observation, Wee declare that a Negro Man, called Salem Poor, of Col. Fryes regiment, Captain Ames company, in the late Battle of Charlestown, behaved like an Experienced officer, as well as an Excellent Soldier, to set forth Particulars of his conduct would be tedious, Wee Would begg leave to say in the Person of this said Negro Centers a brave and gallant soldier. The Reward due so great and Distinguished a Caracter, Wee Submit to Congress. (Brown 1867)

Over 25,000 black troops served the Continental Army (5,000) and the British Army (20,000) on the promise of freedom and a better life ahead. "No regiment is to be seen in which there are not Negroes in abundance and among them are able bodied, strong and brave fellows." (Brown 1867) Neither side really wanted the blacks, but both sides manipulated them to achieve their goals and protect their way of life. The high regard for and fear of Negro troops made them key to victory for either side, as was illustrated by the royal governor of Virginia, John Murray, fourth Earl of Dunmore, whose 7 November 1775 proclamation read that he would free black and white bondsmen who fought for the British. Lord Dunmore's Ethiopian Regiment of 300 slaves were trained and dressed in military uniforms that had "Liberty to Slaves" inscribed on their breasts.

Shocked and fearful of what Lord Dunmore's proclamation would mean on the battlefield, patriot commander Gen. George Washington hastily wrote a letter to Col. Henry Lee, predicting that victory would come to whatever side could arm blacks the fastest and calling for the reenlistment of black freemen who had already served in the army. The reality of troop shortages overcame the fear of rebellion for the Continental army and navy and for the British as well. War is winner take all, and this one was no different. In 1775, Washington, under pressure from the southern colonies, flip-flopped and rejected new enlistment of blacks, although many were already serving in the integrated army and navy. The existing military units were complemented by several segregated ones, like Massachusetts's famous Bucks of America, under the command of Col. George Middleton.

Inset, a detail of the famous John Trumbull painting "The Death of General Warren at the Battle of Bunker Hill" shows Salem and an officer retreating.

"Ain't that funny," Aunt Diskie laughed and hugged herself with secret laughter. "Us got all the advantage, and Old Massa think he got us tied."

—Zora Neale Hurston,
   High John de Conquer

Former slaves and freemen, like James Armistead, born in Virginia in 1748 or 1760, also served as spies for the colonial army. Armistead, with his master's permission, joined the army under the French general the Marquis de Lafayette in 1781. Posing as a slave in the camp of British commander Lord Charles Cornwallis, he relayed information about British troop movements and arms leading to the British defeat at Yorktown. After petitioning the Virginia state legislature for his freedom, and with a letter of commendation from Lafayette in hand in 1784, Armistead received his freedom for his "services and bravery during the siege of Yorktown" in 1786.

Slave/spy James Armistead Lafayette earned his freedom serving the French general Lafayette during the successful siege of Yorktown, Virginia, in 1781, which forced the surrender of Cornwallis's army. *Photo courtesy of Valentine Richmond History Center*

A 1781 engraving of Marquis de Lafayette and James Armistead, who would later take on his master's surname. *Virginia Historical Society, Richmond, Virginia / The Bridgeman Art Library International*

If not serving in Lord Dunmore's Ethiopian Regiment, few blacks fought for Britain in the north or south until late in the war, when 200 black loyalists defended Savannah, Georgia, from attack by the French and Americans in October 1779.

As for the Continental Army, Rhode Island began enlisting slaves in 1778, declaring that "every able-bodied Negro, mulatto, or Indian man slave" that chose to do so and "every slave so enlisting shall, upon his passing muster before Colonel Christopher Greene, be immediately discharged from the service of his master or mistress, and be absolutely free. . . . " Slave owners were compensated for their losses, and the 1st Rhode Island Regiment of 225 men, including 140 blacks, fought in the bloody Battle of Rhode Island in August of 1778. Greene and several of his black troops were ambushed and mutilated by British loyalists in 1781.

As the final British ship left Savannah, Georgia, harbor in July 1782, more than 5,000 slaves departed for Jamaica, St. Augustine, and the West Indies. By 1786, most of those who stayed were back in bondage. The British created a "Book of Negroes" with over three thousand names, and those listed in the book were entitled passage to Nova Scotia, London, and Western Africa. Slaves serving in the Continental Army fared even worse, and Connecticut, Massachusetts, and Southern states had banned blacks from military service by 1785. The United States Congress formally rejected black military service in 1792.

General George Washington crossing the Delaware River in December 1776. Freeman Oliver Cromwell sits at the stroke oar behind Washington's knee. *North Wind Picture Archives via AP Images*

Painting of the Battle of Cowpens, fought in South Carolina in 1780, showing a black trooper firing his pistol at a British officer who is preparing to strike an American officer with his saber.

Antebellum Slave Lore

As the Civil War approached, nearly 4 million slaves were held in a total American population of just over 12 million in the fifteen states where slavery was legal, according to the 1860 U.S. Census. Of all 8,289,782 free persons in the fifteen slave states, 393,967 people (4.8 percent) held slaves, and the average number of slaves held by any single owner was ten. The majority of slaves were held by planters, defined by historians as those who owned twenty or more slaves. Ninety-five percent of black people lived in the South, comprising one-third of the population there, as opposed to comprising 2 percent of the population in the North.

The psychological support of slave humor and music directed against the institution of slavery provided critical support for the oppressed black men, women, and children of America's great disgrace. Humor, widely circulated in early American folklore, has been a coping mechanism of black American culture through good times and bad. The story "Swapping Dreams" offers one such example:

> One morning Master Jim Turner and his slave, Ike, swap dreams. Turner told Ike that he had dreamed he was in "Negro Heaven" and saw garbage in the streets, old torn-down houses, and "a big bunch of dirty Negroes walking around."
>
> "Umph, umph, Massa," said Ike. "You sure must have ate the same thing I did last night, because I dreamed I went to the white man's paradise, and the streets was all of gold and silver, and there was lots of milk and honey there, and pretty gold and pearl gates, but, you know, there wasn't a sole in the whole place."

Examples of music that helped slaves to cope include the Negro spirituals "Wade in the Water," "The Gospel Train," and "Swing Low, Sweet Chariot," each of which directly referred to running away from slavery.

African Warrior in a Box: The Great Slave Escape, 1849

Of all the shocking, savage, and disturbing stories of slavery in America, few are more remarkable than the escape from slavery via U.S. mail by Henry "Box" Brown in 1849. Born into slavery in Louisa County, Virginia, in 1815, Brown worked in a tobacco factory in Richmond in the 1830s. There he met and married his wife, Nancy, and had three children before his family was sold to a slave trader in North Carolina.

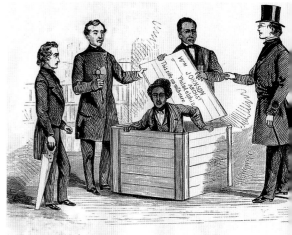

RESURRECTION OF HENRY BOX BROWN.

Illustration to Brown's book.

Devastated by their loss and his inability to prevent it, Brown became obsessed with escaping his slave life. With assistance from freeman James Smith and a white storekeeper named Samuel Smith, Brown conceptualized his escape by U.S. mail. He paid the storekeeper $86, from his savings of $189, for which Smith contacted a white abolitionist in Philadelphia, named James Miller McKim, who agreed to participate in the scheme.

With the determination of an African warrior and in the spirit of the black Union Army soldiers who would help end slavery sixteen years later, Brown began his great escape on 29 March 1849. He packed himself into a two-by-three-foot wood box and literally sent himself on a legendary journey, traveling by wagon, railroad, steamboat, and ferry and finally arriving in Philadelphia twenty-seven hours later. Brown described his ordeal in his 1849 book *Narrative of Henry Box Brown by Himself*:

> I took with me a bladder filled with water to bathe my neck with, in case of too great heat; and with no access to fresh air, excepting three small . . . holes, I started on my perilous cruise. I was first carried to the express office, the box being placed on its end, so that I started with my head downwards, although the box was directed, "this side up with care."
>
> From the express office, I was carried to the depot, and from thence tumbled roughly into the baggage car, where I happened to fall "right side up," but no thanks to my transporters. But after a while the cars stopped, and I was put aboard a steamboat, and placed on my head. In this dreadful position, I remained the space of an hour and a half, it seemed to me, when I began to feel of my eyes and head, and found to my dismay, that my eyes were almost swollen out of their sockets, and the veins of my temple seemed ready to burst.
>
> I made no noise however, determining to obtain "victory or death," but endured the terrible pain, as well as I could, sustained under the whole by the thoughts of sweet liberty. About half an hour afterwards, I attempted again to lift my hands to my face, but I found I was not able to move them.

I made no noise . . . determining to obtain "victory or death" . . . sustained under the whole by the thoughts of sweet liberty.

—Henry "Box" Brown, *Narrative of Henry Box Brown By Himself*

Harriet "Moses" Tubman: The Freedom Train

The slave was treated like a beast. Slavery inseparable from the evil of men; it was God's punishment upon Ham's prurient disobedience. Enslavement was captivity, the loser's lot in a contest of power. Slaves were infidels or heathens. According to the English, on every account, African-Americans qualified.

—W. Jordan, *White Over Black*

Born a slave in Dorchester County, Maryland, as Araminta Ross in 1820, Harriet Tubman immediately experienced the brutal life of a slave. Beaten and molested by a series of slave masters, Tubman was hit by a heavy metal object wielded by another slave, causing a traumatic head wound that would impact her health for the remainder of her life. In addition to suffering disabling seizures, headaches, and spells of hypersomnia, she also experienced dreams and visions that she, a devout Christian, described as premonitions from God.

After escaping to Philadelphia, Pennsylvania, in 1849, she returned to Maryland to rescue her family and began a series of thirteen slave-rescue missions that would free over seventy slaves. She never lost a passenger on her "freedom train." Evading slave bounties and laws, including the Fugitive Slave Law of 1850, Tubman traveled by night through a network of safe houses called the Underground Railroad. Armed with a revolver, she advised her slave "cargo" that she would shoot anyone who tried to turn back. On one mission with a group of fugitive slaves, morale had faded, and one slave vowed to return to his plantation. Tubman responded, "You go on or die!" Several days later, the group successfully entered Canada. Her handgun also came in handy for use against slave owners and their dogs, for defending against snakes, and even for shooting animals for food.

A towering figure in the history of slave rebellion, Harriet Tubman rescued more than seventy slaves via her network of safe houses known as the Underground Railroad. Later, during the Civil War, she helped free hundreds more as a Union scout and spy, and in later years (she lived to be 93) put her energy toward the women's suffrage movement. *Library of Congress*

As the Civil War began, Tubman served the Union Army first as a cook and nurse and later as an armed scout and spy. The first woman to lead an army attack in the war, she guided the Union raid on the Combahee River in South Carolina, freeing over 700 slaves. She also helped John Brown recruit men for his raid on Harpers Ferry and later became a leader in the women's suffrage movement.

A cold sweat now covered me from head to foot. . . . One half hour longer and my sufferings would have ended in that fate, which I preferred to slavery; but I lifted up my heart to God in prayer, believing he would yet deliver me, when to my joy, I overheard two men say, "We have been here two hours and have travelled 20 miles, now let us sit down, and rest ourselves."

They . . . turned the box over, containing my soul and body, thus delivering me from the power of the grim messenger of death, who a few moments previously, had aimed his fatal shaft at my head, and had placed his icy hands on my throbbing heart. One of these men inquired of the other, what he supposed that box contained, to which his comrade replied, that he guessed it was the mail. "Yes," thought I, "it is male, indeed, although not the mail of the United States."

Soon after this fortunate event, we arrived at Washington, where I was thrown from the wagon, and again as my luck would have it, fell on my head. . . . Pretty soon, I heard some one say, "there is no room for this box, it will have to remain behind." I then again applied to the Lord, my help in all my difficulties, and in a few minutes I heard a gentleman direct the hands to place it aboard, as "it came with the mail and must go on with it." I was then tumbled into the car, my head downwards again, as I seemed to be destined to escape on my head. . . .

We had not proceeded far, however, before more baggage was placed in the car, at a stopping place, and I was again turned to my proper position. No farther difficulty occurred until my arrival in Philadelphia. I reached this place at three o'clock in the morning and remained in the depot until six o'clock, A.M., at which time a wagon drove up . . . I was soon placed on this wagon and carried to the house of my friend's correspondent, where quite a number of persons were waiting to receive me.

They appeared to be some afraid to open the box first, but at length one rapped upon it, and with a trembling voice, asked, "Is all right within?" to which I replied, "All right."

The joy of these friends was excessive . . . each one seized hold of some tool and commenced opening my grave. At length the cover was removed and I arose, and shook myself . . . and I swooned away (Stearns 1849, 60–62).

Brown later told his story as a showman in Great Britain for twenty-five years before returning to the United States in 1875, and his cunning escape remains legendary to this day.

A portrait of mixed-race Rev. Lemuel Haynes in New England

Portrait of Agrippa Hull, a freeman from Massachusetts who served with Gen. Thaddeus Kosciuszko in the Continental Army during the war

CHAPTER 2

The Civil War, Western Expansion, and Buffalo Soldiers

This lithograph entitled "Come and Join Us Brothers" was used in 1863 to recruit "colored troops" for the Union cause. It is interesting to note that, as depicted in the lithography, black regiments were almost always commanded by a white officer. *Kean Collection/Getty Images*

William Stephen Morris, JD, who provides the following essay, is an acclaimed author and military historian with a special interest in western lore. The middle son and grandson of two legendary black army officers, lawyers, and publishers, Morris is a graduate of the University of Iowa College of Law and a practicing attorney. His essays have appeared in numerous books and newspapers, including Outside In: African-American History in Iowa, 1830–2000 *(State Historical Society of Iowa, 2000) and the Des Moines Register. Morris has performed extensive research at the Pine Ridge (Lakota/Sioux) Indian Reservation in South Dakota, site of the infamous Wounded Knee massacre in 1890 and the bloody American Indian Movement (AIM) occupation in 1973. An Iowa native, Morris is husband to Amelia, the father of Omar and Stephen Jr. and a life member of Kappa Alpha Psi Fraternity and the Association of the United States Army (AUSA).*

◆ ◆ ◆

Frederick Douglass in 1879. *National Archives*

AFRICAN-AMERICAN MEN have served their country in every war America has engaged in, from the Revolutionary War, where blacks, whites, and Indians fought in integrated militias, through today's global war on terror. During the Civil War, 178,975 black men fought in the Union Army in segregated

A squad of guards from the 107th U.S. Colored Troops at Fort Corcoran in Washington, D.C., 1865. *Library of Congress*

LC-B817- 7861

Band of 107th U.S. Colored Infantry

Once let the black man get upon his person the brass letters "U.S.," let him get an eagle on his button and a musket on his shoulder and bullets in his pockets, and there is no power on earth which can deny that he has earned the right to citizenship.

—Frederick Douglass, 1861

Most African-American troops were noncombatants who performed the least desirable tasks, such as burying the dead, as depicted in this photo of troops burying dead Confederate soldiers taken after the Battle of Antietam in Maryland. *Library of Congress*

units. A further 9,695 served in the integrated U.S. Navy. Of that number, 2,751 black soldiers were killed in action, and 65,427 died of disease or wounds or were listed as missing in action.

Black soldiers participated in 39 major battles and 410 lesser skirmishes. They comprised 135 infantry regiments, 6 cavalry regiments, 12 heavy artillery regiments, and 10 batteries of light artillery. Fifteen states contributed volunteers to the United States Colored Troops (USCT), the official designation given to nearly all black formations in 1864, and the original 54th Massachusetts Infantry Regiment was recruited personally by abolitionist leader Frederick Douglass.

President Abraham Lincoln initially opposed the utilization of black troops in combat, but eventually came to the realization shared by many Union generals: the North's victory in April 1865 could not have been obtained without the service of black soldiers and sailors.

The U.S. War Department issued General Order No. 143 on 22 May 1863, which established the Bureau of Colored Troops. The 1st Kansas Colored Infantry and the 1st South Carolina Colored Regiment were the first two black formations to be recruited and sent into combat. Black soldiers were awarded eighteen Medals of Honor for bravery during the "War of the Rebellion," and another six

Cold Harbor, Virginia: African Americans collect bones of soldiers killed in the battle. *Library of Congress*

Civil War

Twenty-five black Americans earned the Medal of Honor during the Civil War, including U.S. Navy **Landsman Aaron Anderson**, USS *Wyandank*, Mattox Creek, Virginia, 1865, for heroism under fire. The bloody Battle of Chaffin's Farm provided fourteen army medal winners while four sailors received the medal for action at the Battle of Mobile Bay. Navy **Contraband Robert Blake**, USS *Marblehead*, Johns Island, South Carolina, 1863, received the first award in 1864, although **Sgt. William Harvey Carney**, 54th Massachusetts, Battle of Fort Wagner, Morris Island, South Carolina, 1863, performed the first awardable act in 1863 but did not receive the award until 1900.

U.S. Navy Landsman Aaron Anderson, USS *Wyandank*, Mattox Creek, Virginia, 1865, battled the enemy while U.S. Army **Pvt. Bruce Anderson**, 142nd New York Volunteers, led his column under fire at the second Battle of Fort Fisher, North Carolina, 1865.

U.S. Colored Troops **Pvt. William Barnes**, **Sgt. James Harris**, **Sgt. Edward Ratcliff** (38th) , **Sgt. Powhatan Beaty**, **Sgt. James Bronson**, **Sgt. Milton Holland**, **Sgt. Robert Pinn** (5th), **Sgt. Christian Fleetwood**, **Sgt. Alfred Hilton**, **Pvt. Charles Veale** (4th), **Pvt. James Daniel Gardiner**, **Cpl. Miles James** (36th), **Sgt. Maj. Thomas R. Hawkins**, and **Sgt. Alexander Kelly** (6th), all received the medal for action at the Battle of Chaffin's Farm, Virginia, 1864.

Navy **Landsmen William Brown**, **Wilson Brown**, **John Henry Lawson**, and the engineer's cook, **James Mifflin**, USS *Hartford*, all received the medal for their actions at the Battle of Mobile Bay, Alabama, 1864. Navy **Seaman Joachim Pease**, USS *Kearsarge*, showed gallantry under fire off Cherbourg, France, 1864.

William Harvey Carney   James Harris   Powhatan Beaty

U.S. Army **Cpl. Decatur Dorsey**, 39th USCT, rallied his men with the flag at the Battle of the Crater, Petersburg, Virginia, 1864, and **Cpl. Andrew Jackson Smith**, 55th Massachusetts, saved the regimental colors at the Battle of Honey Hill, South Carolina, 1864.

Images: Library of Congress

Milton Holland

Robert Pinn

Christian Fleetwood

James Daniel Gardiner

Thomas R. Hawkins

Alexander Kelly

John Henry Lawson

Andrew Jackson Smith

black sailors were also decorated for bravery. Several white officers in command of black regiments also won the Medal of Honor. Black soldiers comprised nearly half of the Union Army units in the field at the end of the Civil War and fought the last battle of the war against Confederate forces, in Texas.

Young black men, like this drummer boy, joined the Union Army in any capacity they could, taking to heart Frederick Douglass's declaration, "He who would be free must strike the blow." *National Archives*

The battlefield bravery of Medal of Honor recipient Sgt. William H. Carney of the 54th Massachusetts, USCT, illustrates the spirit of black troops during the Civil War:

> In that moment of danger Carney remembered the flag that represented all he held dear and was fighting to protect that day. Rather than dropping the flag and fleeing for his life, he wrapped the flag around the staff to protect it and ran down the embankment. Stumbling through a ditch, chest-deep in water, he held the flag high. Another bullet struck him in the chest, another in the right arm, then another in his right leg. Carney struggled on alone, determined not to let his flag fall to the enemy.
>
> From the safety of distance to which they had retreated, what remained of the valiant warriors of the 54th Massachusetts Colored Infantry watched the brave Sergeant struggle towards safety. A retreating member of the 100th New York passes Carney and, seeing the severity of his wounds said, "Let me carry that flag for you." With indomitable courage Sergeant Carney replied, "No one but a member of the 54th should carry the colors." Despite the sounds of rifle and cannon fire that followed him, Carney wouldn't quit. Amid cheers of his battered comrades Sergeant Carney finally reached safety. Before collapsing among them from his many wounds his only words were, "Boys, I only did my duty. The flag never touched the ground."

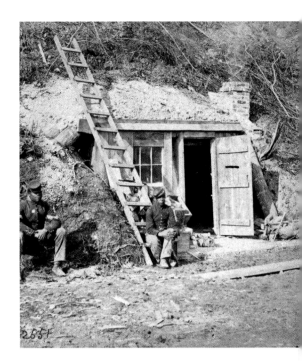

Two African-American soldiers sit in front of the bombproof quarters of Major Thomas J. Strong, 16th New York Heavy Artillery, at Dutch Gap, Virginia. *Ohio Historical Society*

Twenty-one-year-old slave Samuel Cabble served as a private in the 55th Massachusetts Infantry Regiment and was offered for service by his owner. A letter to his slave wife (original spelling, punctuation, and capitalization preserved) reveals his determination to save his wife and country:

> Dear Wife,
>
> I have enlisted in the army I am now in the state of Massachusetts but before this letter reaches you I will be in North Carolina and though great is the present national difficulties yet I look forward to a brighter day When I shall have the opportunity of seeing you in the full enjoyment o freedom I would like to no if you are still in slavery if you are it will not be long before we shall have crushed the system that now opreses you in the course of three months you shall have your liberty. Great is the outpouring of the colered people that is now rallying with the hearts of lions against that very curse that has separated you an me yet we shall meet again and oh what a happy time that will be when this ungodly

rebellion shall be put down and the curses of our land is trampled under our feet I am soldier now and I shall use my utmost endeavor to strike at the rebellion and heart of this system that so long has kept us in chains . . . remain your own affectionate husband until death—Samuel Cabble.

Some 30,000 black men served in various state regiments of the Confederacy and received pensions for their service after the war. Some historians claim there were as many as 6,000 black slave owners in the antebellum South, most of whom contributed funds and supplies to the Confederate war effort. Preston Roberts, a black man, served as unofficial quartermaster general to Confederate general

This nineteenth century hand-colored woodcut illustrates a Confederate charge against African-American Union soldiers at the Battle of the Crater. This division of United States Colored Troops (USCT) under Brig. Gen. Edward Ferrero led the original assault, which took place July 30, 1864.
North Wind Picture Archives via AP Images

54th Massachusetts (Colored) Regiment assaulting Confederate stronghold of Fort Wagner, South Carolina. Hand-colored woodcut of a 19th-century illustration.
North Wind Picture Archives via AP Images

Nathan Bedford Forrest during the war and was awarded the Cross of Gallantry, the Confederacy's highest military decoration. Roberts was buried with full military honors in a white cemetery upon his death in 1910. Forrest would go on to found the Ku Klux Klan at Pulaski, Tennessee, in 1866. In later years, Forrest would try to distance himself from the Klan's terroristic tactics.

U.S. Cavalry patch

Directly due to the solid performance of the soldiers of the various units of the United States Colored Troops during the Civil War, a war-weary Congress authorized the formation of six black regiments for frontier duty, the 9th and 10th cavalries and the 38th, 39th, 40th, and 41st infantry regiments, in 1866. The infantry regiments were consolidated into the 24th and 25th regiments in 1867. Overcoming the prejudice of frontier whites, who stereotyped the black soldiers as disease carriers, cowards, and prone to desertion, the four black regiments went on to distinguished service on the western frontier from 1866 to 1891.

Troopers from the 9th and 10th cavalries would engage and defeat hostiles from the toughest and most rebellious Native American tribes in the west, including the Kiowa, Comanche, Ute, Kickapoo, Arapaho, Apache, Lakota (Sioux), and the northern and southern Cheyenne. Outlaws of all races, cattle rustlers, white slave-trading Comancheros, and bootleg-whisky peddlers were also brought to justice by the Buffalo Soldiers. They were so called because the Indians respected the fighting qualities of the black soldiers, who, like a cornered or wounded buffalo, would fight to the death. The texture of the black soldiers' hair was also similar to the curly mane of the buffalo, which kept the Indians warm during the winter months.

United States marshals, county sheriffs, tax collectors, and other civic officials could not have performed their duties without escort from the Buffalo

Troops of Company E, 4th U.S. Colored Infantry, pose at Fort Lincoln, Washington, D.C., during the Civil War. *Library of Congress*

Picket station near Dutch Gap Canal, November 1864.
Library of Congress

Black soldiers guard a former "slave pen" in Alexandria, Virginia. Alexandria was home to the Franklin & Armfield Slave Market, one of the largest slave trading companies in the country. The building became a jail under Union occupation during the Civil War. *National Archives*

Company B, 25th Infantry, a black regiment that served at Fort Snelling, Minnesota, after the Civil War, seen here in the 1880s. *National Archives*

Soldiers, particularly in Texas, Arizona, New Mexico, and Indian Territory (present-day Oklahoma). Continuity of command and record-high reenlistment rates ensured a large number of experienced veterans in the black regiments. Colonel Edward Hatch led the 9th Cavalry from 1866 until his death in service in 1889. Colonel Benjamin Grierson commanded the 10th cavalry from 1866 to 1890. Colonel Joseph Potter commanded the 24th Infantry for thirteen years. Colonel George Andrews headed the 25th Infantry for twenty-one years. Several white officers who went on to great fame leading white regiments earned their spurs as second lieutenants in the 9th and 10th cavalries, including Wesley Merritt, Albert Morrow, and Ranald "Bad Hand" MacKenzie. The first two black graduates of the U.S. Military Academy at West Point, Lt. Henry Ossian Flipper (1878) and Lt. John Alexander (1887), served with the 10th Cavalry and 9th Cavalry, respectively. Black troopers in the West and in Cuba would earn eighteen Medals of Honor between 1866 and 1898.

Federal soldiers with a wounded black man beside Culpeper Court House, Virginia, September 1863. *Library of Congress*

A black soldier guards a 12-pounder field gun Model 1857—coined the "Napoleon"—at Grant's Headquarters, City Point, Virginia (known today as Hopewell), 1865. *Library of Congress*

Battlefield accomplishments of the Buffalo Soldiers were not their only achievements, as they renovated dozens of army posts, strung thousands of miles of telegraph wire, and escorted stagecoaches, trains, cattle herds, railroad crews, and surveying parties. They opened new roads, prepared maps of large tracts of uncharted territory, and located vital bodies of water for settlers. Discriminatory issue of inferior mounts (condemned horses from white units), rations, and arms and supplies made the accomplishments of the black soldiers all the more notable.

The close of Western expansion and the Wounded Knee massacre in December 1890 brought finality to the Indian Wars. The Buffalo Soldiers played decisive roles in the last two engagements of the Indian campaigns. The 9th Cavalry rode 108 miles nonstop in under twenty-four hours, during a blizzard, to rescue Col. George Forsyth's 7th Cavalry, which was under heavy fire at Drexel Mission during the Wounded Knee incident. The 10th Cavalry performed yeomen service in the

A sketch of a black trooper of the 10th Cavalry serving on the western frontier, ca. 1888. *National Archives*

Southwest against the last Apache fighters, Victorio and Geronimo, resulting in the death of the former at the hands of Mexican troops and the surrender of the latter on 11 September 1886.

The black soldiers' remarkable bravery under fire was due to the troopers' attempts to prove to a racist public that they were not cowards. Historian Robert Utley concluded that "unit pride and espirit de corps ran high in the black regiments, the product in part, of the personnel continuity, but also of increasing professionalism, superior performance, a solidarity born of prejudice, and determination to demonstrate the potential of the black race." (Utley 1973)

Leadership

There were a small number of black officers in the USCT, the highest ranking being Lt. Col. [brevet] Alexander Augusta of South Carolina and Maj. Martin R. Delaney, a graduate of Harvard Medical College. Neither man possessed combat experience. Only the officers of the 1st, 2nd, and 3rd regiments, Louisiana Native Guards, who fought bravely at the Battle of Port Hudson in May 1863, had led men in battle.

Major Francis E. Dumas, executive officer to Col. Nathan W. Daniels, 2nd Regiment, and Capt. Andre Cailloux, killed in action with the 1st Regiment, were this unit's highest-ranking officers. All these men were dismissed from service or resigned their commissions due to racial discrimination by white Union generals in 1864.

This nineteenth century hand-colored woodcut illustrates African-American troops out of the Union Army at Little Rock, Arkansas, after the Civil War. *North Wind Picture Archives via AP Images*

Indian Wars

Of eighteen Medal of Honor recipients during the western Indian Wars, fourteen were "Buffalo Soldiers" from the all-black 9th and 10th Cavalry and the 24th and 25th Infantry regiments. The remaining recipients were Black Seminole scouts on the plains and in Arizona, New Mexico, and Texas, 1866–1890.

U.S. Army **Sgt. Thomas Boyne**, **Sgt. John Denny**, **Cpl. Clinton Greaves**, **Sgt. Henry Johnson**, **Sgt. George Jordan**, **Sgt. Thomas Shaw**, **Sgt. Emanuel Stance**, **Pvt. Augustus Walley**, **1st Sgt. Moses Williams**, **Cpl. William Othello Wilson**, and **Sgt. Brent Woods** represented the 9th Cavalry, while **Sgt. William McBryar** hailed from the 10th Cavalry.

Sgt. Benjamin Brown and **Cpl. Isaiah Mays** represented the 24th Infantry with Seminole scouts **Pfc. Pompey Factor**, **Pvt. Adam Paine**, **Trumpeter Isaac Payne**, and **Sgt. John Ward**.

Images: Library of Congress

John Denny   Thomas Shaw

Brent Woods   William McBryar   Benjamin Brown   Isaiah Mays

Black troops of the 10th Cavalry, seen here posing at Fort Verde, Arizona, also served in Montana during the wars against American Indians on the Great Plains. *Library of Congress*

The 1st Kansas Colored Infantry engaged in combat with Confederate forces at Island Mound, Missouri, in October 1862, claiming the distinction of being the first black regiment to receive their baptism of fire during the Civil War. The 1st South Carolina Colored Regiment was the first unit organized in union service. Despite notable military accomplishments, most black units were relegated to labor duty.

Black Union soldiers were often executed upon surrendering to Confederate forces, as happened most notably at Fort Pillow, Tennessee (1864), after the Battle of the Crater, and at Milliken's Bend, Louisiana. White officers captured leading black troops were also executed, on the spot in many instances, for inciting servile insurrection.

A group of black Seminole scouts, whose tracking skills were essential to the success of the Buffalo Soldiers. *National Archives*

Trumpeters of the 10th Cavalry led their fellow troopers into battle, sounding the charge, retreat, reveille, and taps.

African Methodist Episcopal (AME) Reverend George W. Prioleau, born into slavery in South Carolina and educated at Claflin College and Wilberforce University, was one of the strongest advocates for black men making a career in the U.S. Army. He himself had done so by accepting a chaplaincy in 1894 and serving in the Spanish-American War and at the Fort Des Moines black officers training camp in 1917.

First Lieutenant Henry O. Flipper, the first black graduate of West Point in 1877, served briefly on the frontier with the 10th Cavalry, at Fort Concho, Texas, before resigning his commission due to racial discrimination.
Special Collections, USMA Library

Sergeant Horace W. Bivins was one of the 10th Cavalry's finest soldiers.

The War Department originally allowed discrimination in pay under the Militia Act of 1862, Soldiers of African descent were to be paid $10 a month with $3 deducted for clothing. White privates were paid $13 a month plus a $3 clothing allowance. This outrage was not corrected by Congress until 15 June 1864.

The Union Navy was much more accepting of black servicemen than the army, and allowed integrated combat crews as early as 1862. There was no discrimination in pay between black and white sailors. Nevertheless, blacks could rise no farther than petty officer (a noncommissioned) rank. There would be no black commissioned naval officers until the twentieth century.

Emancipation (1862) and the end of the Civil War in April 1865 launched a tremendous social change in America, during both Reconstruction in the South (1866–1877) and westward expansion. Former members of the USCT would go on to great accomplishments in politics, law, the frontier military (the Buffalo Soldiers), retail business, railroad construction, and law enforcement. Notably, an estimated fifty black U.S. deputy marshals served with distinction in Indian Territory (present-day Oklahoma). Black men served as army scouts, muleskinners, and interpreters for frontier cavalry. Isaiah Dorman, a black woodcutter, interpreter, and army scout, was killed at the Battle of the Little Bighorn on 25 June 1876, under the command of Maj. Marcus Reno. The Civil War, like the Revolutionary War and all

Sergeant George Berry planted the colors of the 3rd Infantry and 10th Cavalry (his unit) on the famous San Juan (Kettle) Hill in Cuba during the Spanish-American War.

armed conflicts since, propelled black Americans ever closer to equality and full citizenship in the United States as no other series of events could or did.

The combat-experienced black soldiers of the 9th and 10th cavalries and the 24th and 25th infantry regiments would rack up an enviable military record from 1866 to 1898. The 9th Cavalry fought a hotly contested battle at Fort Lancaster, Texas, against Kickapoo warriors in 26 December 1867. Outnumbered twenty-to-one, the sixty soldiers of Troop K defeated an estimated 1,200 Kickapoo that besieged the fort.

None other than frontier veteran Elizabeth Bacon Custer, wife of Lt. Col. George Armstrong Custer, commander of the 7th Cavalry, remarked on the performance of black soldiers of the 24th Infantry Regiment. During a surprise attack on Fort Riley, Kansas, in 1867, by an estimated 600 Comanche warriors, the black "walk-a-heaps" (as the Indians called all army infantrymen) counterattacked immediately, chasing the fleeing Indians in horse-drawn supply wagons, as ten soldiers fired in volleys at the Comanches. Mrs. Custer wrote, "The history of the west will not be written without these men . . . "

Veteran black cavalry and infantry units were tasked by the U.S. Army with being the first troops to experiment with early machine guns (the Colt "potato digger") and with bicycles as potential replacements for horses. The

Extraordinary service sometimes won an officer's field commission, as in the case of 2nd Lt. Sant Foster of the 10th Cavalry.

Company of the 24th Infantry Regiment, a colored infantry unit that supported the 10th Cavalry, Cuba, 1898. *National Archives*

accomplishments of the black cavalry were even more commendable given the inferior horses they were issued by the army; these horses were usually wind-blown, broken-down mounts from white units, and some of them had even pulled artillery caissons.

Sergeant George Berry of the 10th Cavalry carried the colors and led black and white soldiers up San Juan (Kettle) Hill during the Spanish-American War. Black soldiers were the first to seize the heights of the hill from Spanish riflemen and run the American flag up the flagpole in the Spanish garrison. Five Medals of Honor were awarded to black soldiers for bravery in Cuba. Roughrider commander and future president Theodore Roosevelt would claim, "A bond exists between us, black and white officers and enlisted men, a tie I trust that will never be broken."

Spanish-American War

Six black Americans, named "Smoked Yankees" by the Spanish, received the medal during the Spanish-American War in 1898. **Sgt. Maj. Edward Baker Jr.** saved troops at Santiago, while **Pvt. Dennis Bell**, **Pvt. Fitz Lee**, **Pvt. William Thompkins**, and **Pvt. George Wanton** represented the 10th Cavalry with bravery at Tayabacoa, Cuba. Navy **Fireman 1st Class Robert Penn**, USS *Iowa*, bravely fought fire off Santiago de Cuba, 1898, and saved the battleship from destruction.

Non-combat

U.S. Navy seamen dominated non-combat recipients of the Medal of Honor prior to World War II, when the criteria limited the nominees to combat personnel only. Almost all the actions were for saving fellow seamen from drowning. All African-American non-combat recipients served in the nineteenth century: **Seamen Daniel Atkins**, USS *Cushing*, 1898; **John Davis**, USS *Trenton*, 1881; **Alphons Girandy**, USS

Edward Baker Jr. Robert Penn

Petrel, 1901; **John Johnson**, USS *Kansas*, 1872; **William Johnson**, USS *Adams*, 1879; **Joseph Noil**, USS *Powhatan*, 1872; **John Smith**, USS *Shenandoah*, 1880; and **Robert Augustus Sweeney** (2), USS *Kearsarge*, 1881, and USS *Jamestown*, 1884.

Images: Library of Congress

The 10th Cavalry in mounted review, 1886. *National Archives*

A student at Hampton Institute (now Hampton University in Virginia) reads to an elderly couple. Hampton received much of its early financial support after the Civil War from former officers and soldiers of the Union Army. Among the school's famous alumni is Booker T. Washington. *U.S. Army*

CHAPTER 3

World War I: Black Officers and the New Negroes

U.S. Army infantry troops, African-American unit, marching northwest of Verdun, France, in World War I. *Library of Congress*

THEY STOOD SIDE-BY-SIDE at attention as the greatest assembly of black intellect in American history. One thousand black college graduates and faculty of prestigious institutions of higher learning, ranging from historically black Howard and Tuskegee to Ivy League Harvard and Yale, and 250 noncommissioned officers (NCOs) from the famous 10th Cavalry Buffalo Soldiers and the 24th Infantry Regiment had traveled to Fort Des Moines, Iowa, which was a deserted cavalry post.

George H. Woodson was a Howard University law graduate in 1896 and served as a noncommissioned officer (NCO) with the U.S. Army 25th Infantry on the Plains. He became camp advisor to Col. Charles Ballou. In 1905, Woodson cofounded the Niagara Movement, which became the National Association for the Advancement of Colored People (NAACP) in 1909. After receiving a doctorate in law degree in 1917, he would go on to cofound the National Bar Association in 1925, becoming its first national president.

With less than thirty days notice the superb youth, the very best brain, vigor, and manhood of the Race gave up comfort, position, future promise and outlook, in their various civil locations, and from the North, South, East and West, started on their voluntary march to Fort Des Moines to answer the call . . . God grant their efforts and sacrifices may open a brighter and better day for all the downtrodden people of the earth and especially the oppressed colored people of these United States.

—George H. Woodson,
noncommissioned officer,
U.S. Army 25th Infantry

Although the cadets were all committed to making segregationist president Woodrow Wilson's Great Experiment succeed, jealousy soon arose on the part of the technically brilliant, but academically illiterate NCOs from the plains regiments toward the highly educated college men, whom the military men labeled as "ninety-day wonders." According to cadet James B. Morris, "They [the NCOs] were great post soldiers who could show you how to disassemble and reassemble a machine gun but could not tell you how to do it."

By the time they received their commissions in October 1917, only 639 would remain, and they were dispersed to enlisted camps across America, including Camp Dodge, Iowa, where the 366th Infantry would be formed. News of race riots at enlisted camps in Illinois and Texas in 1917 and a racially charged army hanging of black troops at Camp Dodge the following summer strained race relations across the United States, but the new black officers clung tight to their dream. Morris recalled:

> Our commander, Col. [Charles C.] Ballou, issued an order to the locals that "if anyone discriminated against his cadets, he would place the town under marshal law." He dined with the town leaders that night at the Des Moines Club and got a washing down, and the next day reversed himself. He told us that 'If you want to

This Iowa Boys group photograph includes three National Bar Association founders: Samuel Joe Brown, James Morris, and Charles Howard. *History & Views*

This lawyers association included future National Bar Association (1925) cofounders Brown, Howard, and Morris. The National Bar Association is now a 40,000-member international legal organization. *History & Views*

World War I soldier, half-length portrait, seated, facing front, with two hats on table.
Library of Congress

Ralph Waldo Tyler (1859–1921), Columbus, Ohio, newspaper reporter and editor, government official, essayist, and sole official African-American war correspondent during World War I. *Ohio Historical Society*

be good and recognized, you've got to make yourself so good and desirable that people would seek you and cease that kind of talk.

Although news arrived of race riots at enlisted camps, our only trouble was with one fellow from Boston they called a "tree man." He was standing right behind a company commander who inquired to another, "How is your tree man getting along?" The tree man was a hot head, and the resulting fight was the talk of the camp for a while. (Morris 1975)

In addition to the tree-man fight, Colonel Ballou worried that the black cadets would eventually clash with the surrounding white community, so he devised a plan to put white fears at ease. On 22 July, he assembled the cadets at Drake University stadium to march and sing Negro spirituals for 10,000 curious spectators, and the White Sparrow program, as it was called, was a big hit.

Another step Ballou took to avoid racial conflict was to establish a post YMCA, where the cadets could relax, write letters home, and stay clear of potential social problems like interacting with the local ladies. The post YMCA was run by white secretary R. B. DeFrantz from Kansas City, Missouri, and black assistant secretary W. H. J. Beckett from Washington, D.C.

"It [the YMCA] has actively co-operated with the Camp Commander in every instance that opportunity was afforded it in the work of establishing and maintaining among the candidates a proper spirit and attitude with regard to every difficulty that threatened the welfare of the camp," wrote Colonel Ballou. "Its influence in

World War I

In spite of incredible combat heroics by the black 92nd and 93rd divisions across France, only one Medal of Honor was awarded to a black soldier in the First World War. **Corporal Freddie Stowers**, 371st Infantry, 93rd Division, led his squad to destroy the enemy before being killed up Hill 188, Champagne Marne Sector, France, 1918. He did not receive his medal until an army investigation in 1990 leading to its award in 1991, nearly 73 years after his service.

The grave marker of Freddie Stowers at the Meuse-Argonne American Cemetery and Memorial east of Romagne-sous-Montfaucon in France, near the border with Belgium. *U.S. Army*

Major Charles Young of the 10th Cavalry, just prior to being made lieutenant colonel, 1916. *National Archives*

Bert Williams sings a psalm at the first regimental open air service for the 15th Regiment of the New York National Guard, held in Olympic Field, 136th Street and Fifth Avenue, New York City, 1914. *Library of Congress*

Group portrait of World War I volunteers for active duty. *National Archives*

such instances, happily few, was very considerable, and was always cast on the right side. Too much credit cannot be given the Secretary, Mr. DeFrantz, and his big-hearted volunteer worker, Dr. Cabaniss." (Thompson 1917)

On 15 October 1917, the first black commissioned-officer candidate class in U.S. military history received their commissions as the 17th Provisional Training Regiment, creating a legacy of leadership, service, and honor that is followed to this day. Although three blacks had previously graduated from the U.S. Military Academy at West Point, New York, the 1,250 officer candidates at Fort Des Moines, Iowa, in 1917 represented the army's first real effort to integrate its leadership ranks. President Woodrow Wilson and Secretary of War Newton Baker grudgingly supported the camp, although much of the military establishment opposed the concept of black commissioned officers, and the obscure cavalry post in Iowa was selected over Howard University in Washington, D.C., to host what many whites believed would be a total failure and embarrassment to the army and the nation. The graduating 639 captains and lieutenants from Fort Des Moines dispersed to basic-training posts, including Camp Dodge, Iowa, where the 366th Infantry was formed.

Black troops from the 365th, 366th, 367th, and 368th infantry regiments were ordered overseas on 19 May 1918 and deployed to France from Hoboken, New Jersey, on 10 June. Formed into the 92nd Division, the black soldiers arrived at Brest (Finisterre), France, on 19 June and began training at Bourbonne-les-Bains at Haute Marne.

Ordered into the Saint Die Line on 21 August, the 92nd relieved the white 6th Infantry and French 33rd Corps. It was attacked by the Germans at Frappelle on 25 August and again, with brutal hand-to-hand combat, on the 31 August. The Germans attacked again at Ormont on 1 September and were again repulsed by the 92nd, and the black troops witnessed their first aerial duel overhead at Raon L'Etape on 15 September. Under constant fire, the aggressive 92nd patrols took German prisoners and had two men captured on 15 September, prompting the enemy to drop its first race-propaganda pieces.

After twenty-eight days in the Saint Die sector, the 92nd were ordered to the Argonne Forest, arriving 23 September after a 300-mile train ride. The 368th suffered 450 casualties advancing against the Germans, and with the 366th took Le Chemin.

92nd Infantry Division patch

Black nursing students march to the dining room at Hampton Institute, Virginia, 1916. *U.S. Army*

Panoramic view of the White Sparrow patriotic ceremony at Drake University stadium on 22 July 1917. All 1,250 cadets marched and sang Negro spirituals for 10,000 spectators, demonstrating harmlessness toward the white community. *History & Views*

Charged with building a road across no-man's-land under heavy fire, the 365th, the 366th, and 317th Engineers completed the mission with minimal casualties.

On 5 October 1918, the 92nd was ordered to the Marbache River section and began a bloody northern advance toward the German fortress at Metz. From the Saint Die Line to Meuse-Argonne, the 92nd fought with ferocity and bravery, and their action culminated with the Battle of Metz, France, from 9 to 11 November 1918 against the formidable German fortress. This was the first major battle spearheaded by black troops under the command of black officers in U.S. military history. Their success was summarized by their commanding officer, Maj. Gen. Charles C. Ballou, on 18 November 1918:

> Five months ago today, the 92nd Division landed in France. After seven weeks of training, it took over a sector [Saint Die] in the front line, and since that time some portion of the Division has been continuously under fire.

Mess attendants, USS *Bushnell*, 1918. *U.S. Army*

Members of Training Company 5 study at school desks at Fort Des Moines, Iowa. In addition to rigorous physical training, a complicated classroom schedule kept the cadets busy throughout the ninety-day camp. *History & Views*

Panoramic view of graduate captains, with commissions in hand, at Fort Des Moines on 15 October 1917. These officers would lead the 92nd Division in World War I France after basic training at various locations across the nation, including Camp Dodge, Iowa, where the famed 366th Infantry Regiment was formed. *State Historical Society of Iowa*

It participated in the last battle of the war [Metz] with credible success, continually pressing the attack against highly organized defensive works. It advanced successfully on the first day of the battle, attaining its objectives and capturing prisoners . . . in the face of determined opposition by an alert enemy, against rifle, machine-gun and artillery fire.

May the future conduct of every officer and man be such as to reflect credit upon the Division and upon the Colored race (Scott 1919).

Black soldiers also served valiantly under French command in what was informally called the 93rd Division, which had arrived in France prior to the 92nd on New Year's Day, 1918. The New York 15th National Guard Regiment, which became the 369th Infantry Regiment, was led by five black commissioned officers, including Lt. James Reece Europe. Led by white colonel William Hayward, the four national guard regiments included the 15th Old New York "Hell Fighters"

(the 369th), the Old 8th Illinois "Black Devils" (370th), and the 371st and 372nd "Red Hand" regiments, all of whom would later receive the signal honor of the French *Croix de Guerre* medal and all of whom formed what was called the Rainbow Division. Black combat heroes, like privates Henry Johnson and Needham Roberts, became the first Allied troops to win the Croix de Guerre.

The first Allied force to reach the Rhine River, the 369th, adopted the name *Black Watch*. They had withstood German fire for 191 days and prompted Hayward to boast, "My men never retire. They go forward, or they die." In fact, the 369th Division's impressive combat record included never having a man captured, although the Germans killed over 200 and wounded 800 more. Conversely, the 369th Division's 3rd Battalion alone captured 400 Germans and killed and wounded countless enemy troops. A captured Prussian officer quipped, "We can't hold up against these men. They are devils! They smile while they kill and won't be taken alive." (Scott 1919)

So proud were the troops of the 369th that they complained when their five black officers, who had arrived in France with them, were transferred to the black-commanded 92nd Division, a move that prompting Hayward to issue an explanation:

> In August 1918, the American Expeditionary Force adopted the policy of having either all-white or all-colored officers with Negro regiments, and so ours were shifted away (though Lt. Europe later was returned to us as bandmaster, whereas he had been in the machine gun force before). Our colored officers were in the July fighting and did good work, and I then and feel now, that if colored officers are available and capable, they, and not white officers, should command colored troops. I hope, if the 15th is reconstructed, as it should be, colored men will have the active work or officering it, from top to bottom. . . .

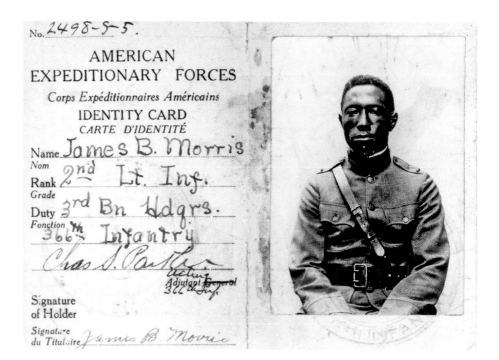

Identification card of Lt. James Morris, American Expeditionary Force, 3rd Battalion, 92nd Division, 366th Infantry, France, 1918. Morris, a Howard University–educated lawyer, served as an intelligence officer, forward scout, and sniper, surviving two combat wounds. He went on to cofound the National Bar Association in 1925; cofound the National Newspaper Publishers Association (NNPA), America's first national black legal and media network, in 1940; and publish the *Iowa Bystander* (founded 1894), the oldest black newspaper west of the Mississippi River, from 1922 to 1972.

There is splendid materiel there. I sent away 42 sergeants in France who were commissioned officers in other units. I would have sent others, but they declared that they'd rather be sergeants in the 15th than lieutenants or captains in other regiments (Scott 1919).

The New Negroes

In addition to victories on the battlefield, the World War I black troops made another major contribution to European culture. The highly educated officers of the 92nd Division presented a direct contradiction to the racist, European-colonial concept of primitivism, and musicians of the 93rd Division's 369th and 370th infantry regiments had an impact all their own. Labeled *New Negroes*

Big Nims of the 92nd Division, 366th Infantry, laughs as fellow soldier tries on his gas mask in France, 1918. Mustard gas was a feared cause of death for the soldiers in the trenches, and the ability to put on the gas mask under fire often proved the difference between life and death. *Scott's History*

Decorated officers of the 92nd Division strut their stuff in France, in 1918, after Battle of Metz before embarking for the United States. From left to right are Lt. C. L. Abbott (South Dakota); Capt. Jos Lowe (California); Lt. A. R. Fisher (Indiana), winner of the Distinguished Service Cross; and Capt. E. White (Arkansas). The highly educated officers would return stateside and survive the infamous Blood Red Summer of 1919 to anchor America's first black middle class of the 1920s. *Scott's History*

by the French and cruising on the sounds of jazz music provided by army regimental bands, the love for black culture known as "Negrophilia" (Archer-Straw 2000) permeated every aspect of French life, from music and art to fashion and interracial relations, between 1918 and 1935.

Black military musical groups, like Lt. James Reece Europe's fabulous Hell Fighters Band of the 369th Infantry (New York 15th National Guard

Enlisted troops of the American Expeditionary Force (AEF) 93rd Division, 369th Infantry, show their Croix de Gerre medals before embarkation home. Serving under French command, the 369th Infantry had served in France since early 1918. *Scott's History*

Regiment); the Black Devils Band of the 370th Infantry, led by Lt. George Dulf; and the 350th Field Artillery Band, led by Lt. J. T. Brymm, became so popular that French and American generals competed for their time, and the public devoured every note of what star musician Lt. Noble Sissle called the "jazz germ." All the regiments of the 92nd also had bands. Their effect was described by Charles Welton:

The [French] audience could stand it no longer, the "Jazz germ" hit them, and it seemed to find the vital spot, loosening all muscles and causing what is known in America as an "Eagle Rocking Fit." "There now," I said to myself. "Colonel Haywood has brought his band over here and started ragtimitis in France; ain't

The 369th Regimental Band "jazzed its way through France" and filled up all the vacant spaces in "No Man's Land" with the remnants of notes broken by the shells and shrapnel as the one hundred master "jazzers" forced their lines to the very banks of the Rhine, where the world woke up and found them on the day the armistice was signed.

—Charles Welton,
World Magazine, 30 March 1919

A Soldier Coming Home

I never thought I would live to see the day when I could stand up on my hind legs and walk and talk like a man.

— Lt. James W. Mitchell, 1975

Lieutenant James Wardlaw Mitchell (1892–1979) was a Georgia native and a graduate of Morris Brown College who had enlisted for the first U.S. Army officer candidate class at Fort Des Moines, Iowa, in 1917. He survived bloody combat in World War I in France with the 92nd Division, 350th Machine Gun Battalion, in 1918, returning to Georgia during the Blood Red Summer of 1919 and attempting to surprise his minister father upon his arrival.

Mitchell had been born to Rev. Wigner Mitchell and Cecilia Haskett-Mitchell in Harrison, Georgia, in 1892. His father was a Methodist preacher across southwestern Georgia, where young James "picked wild berries, trapped quail, and picked up old snake skins near river bottoms and sold them for ten cents a dozen for a little money. . . . " In spite of a hot temper and intolerance for racial discrimination that nearly got him lynched on a number of occasions across the Deep South, Mitchell had recently graduated Morris Brown College in Atlanta in 1916 when he and fellow student Walter White (a future NAACP director) heard an army general give an inspiring recruitment speech.

"He said, 'We are going across the water, and we're going to lick the Huns, " Mitchell told an interviewer in 1975. " 'Then when we come back, there'll be no black people, there'll be no brown people, there'll be no white people. We will all be just people.' I asked Walter, 'You believe what that man says?' I said, 'Let's go,' and we marched right down to the Capitol and signed up. Then we took these tests, mental and written, and later physical examinations to qualify us (Walter failed), and I was soon on the train to Fort Des Moines."

After graduating officer-candidate training at Fort Des Moines, Iowa, and basic training at Camp Dodge, Iowa, Mitchell embarked for France in May of 1918. His 20 February 1975 account of his war experience is as follows.

After the great drive, I was sent back to Lorraine to pick up wounded soldiers who could return to the line. And although the town was pretty much shot up, there were still a lot of businesses open. The Café Lorraine was racially segregated, so I went in Café Del Hemisphere, where I found black and white American soldiers and French soldiers

Morris and Mitchell are seen here in 1975, when they toured Fort Des Moines, where they completed officer training in 1917. Both survived bloody combat in France, where Morris was wounded twice with the 366th Infantry and Mitchell the 350th Machine Gun Battalion.

mingling together, drinking and having fun. I walked in, and a little French girl noticed me and took me to a table where three white American officers sat, and she thought I would be welcome. I started to sit down, and one guy turned and started looking out the window. But the others introduced themselves and said they were from Wisconsin. I said that I appreciate their welcome, but don't want to break up their party, and I will find another table. They said, "No you don't. You're gonna sit right here."

Pretty soon the window looker stood up. He says, "Gentlemen, I have been a fool . . . I want to apologize," and we toasted with champagne. He says, "I was born and raised in Louisiana, and they taught me down there that Negroes weren't any better than dogs. I find they are better than dogs." He called me brother, shook my hand, and greeted me, and I corresponded with that fellow for a long time. He says, "I am a teacher back in Louisiana, and if I get back, I'll teach the kids that Negroes are better than dogs." Well, that was quite an experience because I think he was convinced.

General Melvin Hill Bond was a friend of mine who called me by name every time he saw me. We were attacking from these mountains as the Germans were coming up the valley, and we turned our biggest machine guns on them, which swept them back. Soon afterwards, I was out in the trenches, trying to see what dead I could. I felt a hand on my shoulder and looked around, and there was General Bond, who was one of the few generals who ventured into the front lines. He says, "Hi, Mr. Mitchell. How are you getting along up here?" I says, "Well, it's kind of rough sometimes, but we take care of ourselves." He says, "That's the spirit, that's the spirit." He was without staff,

Group portrait of an officer training company at Fort Des Moines. The cadets stayed dedicated to their mission, although nearly half would be dismissed or leave before commissions were received in October 1917. *History & Views*

and his horse was nearby, and I don't think he realized he was in a very dangerous spot.

At Belleau Wood, our machine-gun outfit held the left flank for the attacking Marines. Don't tell me the American soldier is no hero. I was right there and saw it happen. Belleau Wood changed hands six or seven times in one day. The Germans would drive the Marines out, and the Marines would strike and drive the Germans out, and it ended up in American hands as both sides lost a lot of men. There wasn't a tree standing when they got done with that heavy artillery.

The treatment we [black troops] received from the French people was indescribable as I didn't think that could happen to a black person. They [French] would take you into their homes and do anything for you. I was made town mayor. Whenever my company went into a town, I became the American mayor and lived in the mayor's home.

One French mayor asked me to come to his office one day, and he produced a pamphlet and little brochure. It said, "We white Americans do not appreciate the fact that you are accepting Negroes as social equals." It went on to say how inferior we [blacks] were in all sorts of things, and I told him this was prejudice and he responded, "No, it's jealousy."

One day I was walking down the street in Santia, reminding myself that I came over here to fight Germans, not Americans, when I encountered a lanky white enlisted soldier from the Wildcat Division of South Carolina. He stopped and looked at me and said, "What is this?" He didn't salute, and I got mad. As we passed, I turned around and hollered at him, and he straightened up. I told him to get to attention, with my hand resting on my side arm. I asked him what army he belonged to. "Do they teach you to salute officers when you meet them?" I said. He responded that they didn't have to salute Niggers, and I told him that as long as I wear this uniform, you better salute or face big trouble. I took off my coat and hung it on a picket fence and made him salute it with a cadence for ten minutes. I then turned him over to a Negro MP [military police officer] to take to his commanding officer, and I never heard any more about it.

One day I saw a Senegalese [black] officer commanding a white French company, and they respected him, which was so different from what you would see in America. The 600,000 French colonial subjects had saved France in many battles, and the Germans were afraid of them. The Senegalese officer was tall and dark, with a ring in his ear, and spoke with a heavy voice. In my feeble French, I asked, "You a Negro aren't you?" He said he was, but added, "You no good because you come from slaves!" Can you imagine that? The American Negro today is the most enlightened Negro in the world, but he's also the most hated and despised.

Three days after the armistice, in the town of Nancy, French women were walking the streets with champagne

Black troops arrive by train in Hoboken, New Jersey, for deployment to France as the AEF, 3rd Battalion, 92nd Division, in 1918. The black soldiers would be refused landing by Great Britain and instead travel directly to France. *National Archives*

General John "Black Jack" Pershing, supreme commander of the AEF, decorates troops of the 92nd Division in France, in 1918. The 92nd Division would be tested at Meuse-Argonne sector and the final Battle of Metz, where the unit ended the war by attacking the German fortress. *National Archives*

bottles in their hands, stark naked, just crying and carrying on. They were so happy the Americans had saved them and offering us pleasure as a reward. After the war ended, like many black soldiers, I tried unsuccessfully to stay in France, as returning stateside to Georgia was certain to be a dangerous adventure.

My father, the Reverend Mitchell, was a Methodist circuit preacher living in Milledgeville, the old state capital of Georgia, and my attempt to surprise him failed as I was told he had traveled to Barnesville to speak at a small church. Barnesville was about fifty miles south of Atlanta.

I traveled down there to spend an hour or two with my dad and arrived between 1 and 2 p.m., but was told by the local minister that my father had spoken at the morning services and had gone back to Milledgeville. I was disappointed that I had missed him, and the train back to Atlanta did not leave until 5 p.m.

The pastor told me he had never seen a Negro officer and asked if I would speak at his afternoon services. I told him, "Man, I ain't no speaker . . . I'm just a hard-headed soldier." He responded, "Well, I don't think this will be a spellbinder, but just to see you would be a great inspiration for my congregation." I agreed to do the best I could.

I got up and talked about the war and how I commanded men and my experience in the army. When I concluded, I made a statement [that] was an error. I said that in my travels in the army, I had covered twenty to twenty-five thousand miles. I had the privilege of rubbing shoulders with men from every corner of the globe. The most damnable creature I've met throughout my travels is the Southern cracker!

The pastor got up and ran out of the church, and nobody said amen, but instead the congregation started moaning and groaning. I asked the deacon what was the matter with

The French colonial empire sent 600,000 Senegalese soldiers to fight against the Germans in World War I. *Scott's History*

these people, and he said, "I'll tell you the truth," and I followed him outside. An old man came over and said, "Son, I know the stuff that you said up there was true, but I think you used poor judgment. You better leave town right away." He continued that, "Some of these Negroes are going up to tell the white folks what you said, and they'll do something about it."

I told the old man that I have faced life and death many times, and I'm not afraid now. My train leaves at 5 p.m., and when my train leaves I will be leaving.

We arrived at the train station before 5 p.m., and I was standing on the platform in full uniform with medals on my chest and my pistol in my pocket. They [whites] lingered around and looked in my direction, and when my train came, I went on back.

On Wednesday morning, I got a letter from the pastor that said a [white] mob had touched every Negro home in Barnesville looking for me that night. They wanted to lynch me. I guess I was lucky to get out of there. (Mitchell 1975)

Lieutenant James Reece Europe's fabulous Harlem Hellfighters Band introduced jazz music to France, sparking the avant-garde European cultural revolution during and after World War I. *National Archives*

this an awful thing to visit upon a nation with so many burdens?" But when the band had finished and the people were roaring with laughter, their faces wreathed in smiles, I was forced to say that this is just what France needs at this critical moment.

Later paralleling the Harlem (New York) Renaissance, the army bands were followed by a parade of black American artists, ranging from entertainers Josephine Baker and Paul Robeson to poet Langston Hughes, all of whom were treated as royalty by their newfound French countrymen and women, in a direct contradiction to American racial segregation (Archer-Straw 2000).

"If France was well supplied with American bands, playing their lively tunes, I'm sure it would help a good deal in bringing home entertainment to our boys,

Europe and his band were so popular with white American and French generals that the officers fought over their services. *National Archives*

Europe, and the American artists that followed, sparked a fire in Parisians that engulfed many of their most prominent residents, including shipping heiress Nancy Cunard and artist Pablo Picasso. *National Archives*

and at the same time make the heart of sorrow-stricken France beat a deal lighter," wrote Welton in 1918.

Many black army veterans returned to France in 1919 and married French women while experiencing a mixed bag of relations with the war-weary Europeans. The hot jazz clubs of Paris and the social freedoms of its society provided black soldiers an attractive alternative to the Jim Crow segregation of the southern United States and the racist horror experienced by many of their returning comrades during the "Blood Red Summer" of 1919.

In this 1918 photograph, Lt. Charles Howard of the AEF, 3rd Battalion, 92nd Division, 366th Infantry, shows off his tailored uniform, which was made in France. A Drake University–educated lawyer and Fort Des Moines officer candidate school graduate, Howard would cofound the National Bar Association in 1925 and become the National Black Press correspondent to the United Nations for many years.

James B. Morris graduates from Hampton Institute, Virginia, in 1912. After graduating from Howard University Law School, in Washington, D.C., in 1915, he enlisted for officer training at Fort Des Moines, Iowa, in 1917, later leading the 366th Infantry in World War I France. Note the Union Army uniforms worn by Hampton students in 1912.

World War I Army Lynching at Camp Dodge

Lt. J. B. Morris' all-black 366th Infantry Regiment had deployed to France in May 1918, when on 5 July, three black soldiers were hung for "assaulting and outraging" a 17-year-old white girl at the Camp Dodge, Iowa, post on 24 May. With the entire 88th "Alabama enlisted regiment" standing at attention. Alabama enlisted troops Robert Nelson Johnson (Tuscamba), Stanley Tramble (Stroud), and Fred Allen (Georgiana), were hung in front of their unarmed black peers while armed white guards stood by. The death sentence had been confirmed by segregationist President Woodrow Wilson.

According to an article appearing in the July 6, 1918, edition of the *New York Times*, "Newspapermen were the only civilians admitted. Every [black] soldier in the division not assigned to other duty was ordered to attend the hanging. . . . Three Negro soldiers among the spectators fainted when the men dropped to their death and another ran amuck."

The alleged victim, a 17-year-old white girl and telephone operator at the camp, was brought on the post by her white fiancée Pvt. Gustafeson and claimed the Negroes beat her boyfriend and molested her. According to the July 1918 edition of the *Camp Dodger* (Camp Dodge, Iowa), the black troopers responded that "they had paid the white girl money and the assault was committed with her consent" to no avail as the all-white military court sentenced them to death.

Officers of the 92nd Division pose in France, 1918. *Scott's History*

The poetry of the day told their story, such as the following two examples, "Our Dead," composed by Oliver Wendell Holmes, and "The Fallen Hero," by Minna Irving.

Our Dead

Not with the anguish of hearts that are breaking
Come we as mourners to weep for our dead;
Grief in our breast has grown weary of aching,
Green is the turf where are tears we have shed.

While o'er their marbles the mosses are creeping,
Stealing each name and its legend away,
Give their proud story to memory's keeping,
Shrined in the temple we hallow today.
Hushed are the battlefields. Ended their marches.
Deaf are their ears to the drum beats of mourn—
Rise from the sod, ye fair columns and arches;
Tell their bright deeds to the ages unborn!

Emblem and legend may fade from the portal,
Keystone may crumble and pillar may fall;
They were the builders whose work was immortal,
Crowned with the dome that is over us all (Scott 1919).

The Fallen Hero

He went to the war in the morning—
The roll of the drums could be heard,
But he paused at the gate with his mother,
For a kiss and a comforting word.
He was full of the dreams and ambitions
That youth is so ready to weave,
And proud of the clank of his saber
And the chevrons of gold on his sleeve.

He came from the war in the evening—
The meadows were sprinkled with snow,
The drums and the bugles were silent
And the steps of the soldiers were slow.
He was wrapped in the flag of his country
When they laid him away in the mould,
With the glittering bars of a captain
Replacing the chevrons of gold.

With the heroes who slept on the hillside
He lies with a flag on his head,
But, blind with the tears of her weeping,
His mother yet mourns for her dead.
The soldiers who fall in battle
May feel but a moment of pain,
But the women who wait in the homesteads
Must dwell with the ghosts of the slain (Scott 1919).

CHAPTER 4

World War II:
Black Women at War

Proud black WAAC troops at Fort Des Moines in 1943 pose with new uniforms. Many had been forced to wear men's clothing until their uniforms arrived. *U.S. Army*

Black members of the Women's Army Auxiliary Corps (WAAC) under inspection by Lt. Charity Adams at Fort Des Moines, Iowa, 1942. *State Historical Society of Iowa*

TWENTY-FIVE YEARS after the army's first black officer class arrived at Fort Des Moines, Iowa, the first black female officer candidates in U.S. military history stood at attention on the same spot with the purpose of "making available to the national defense the knowledge, skill, and special training of the women of the nation." (Bellafaire 1994)

Bracing for the impact of black female officers and a potential negative reaction from the military establishment and public, the army made its stance clear from the beginning in 1942: "There will be no discrimination in the type of duties to which Negro women in the WAAC may be assigned . . . Every effort will be made through intense recruiting to obtain the class of colored women desired, in order that there may be no lowering of the standard in order to meet ration requirements." (Bellafaire 1994)

On 29 August 1942, the first 39 black female officers of 440 total cadets, like the men in 1917, would win their commissions at Fort Des Moines, Iowa, and begin a proud legacy of female leadership of America's armed forces. However, the first, second, and third officers (captains and first and second lieutenants) could not command men and drew less pay than their male counterparts. The women in the auxiliaries, as the women's units were called, were also denied the overseas

You are the example of free women defending a free way of life, to the exclusion of everything else, until the war is won . . . Hope and history join here. The women of the United States are saying . . . We shall not fail freedom.

—Lt. Col. Oveta Culp Hobby, Women's Army Auxiliary Corps (WAAC) Director, 1942

Lieutenant Earl Shepperd and Nurse Ellen Robinson at Fort Huachuca, Arizona, 1942. *U.S. Army*

I was very happy that day. The fact that I had been the first Negro woman to receive a commission in the WAAC was nearly as impressive as the fact that "we had arrived." Whatever doubts we might have later, that day we knew ourselves as members of the great fraternity of officers.

—Lt. Charity E. Adams, first WAAC commissioned officer, 1942

pay, life insurance, veterans' medical coverage, and death benefits given to army men. As part of the original Women's Army Auxiliary Corps (WAAC), they joined 7,000 female commissioned officers and 65,000 enlisted troops who would train at Fort Des Moines between 1942 and 1945, comprising half of all WAAC troops trained during World War II. The brainchild of U.S. Congresswoman Edith Nourse Rogers, the bill that created the WAAC was ignored until the Japanese bombed Pearl Harbor in December 1941. U.S. Army chief of staff Gen. George C. Marshall argued with opponents that the army could ill afford to spend the time and money necessary to train men in essential service skills such as typing and switchboard operations when highly skilled women were available. (Bellafaire 1994) The corps was renamed the Women's Army Corps (WAC) in 1943, and the women would serve in noncombat roles throughout World War II Europe and the South Pacific.

The 118 black female commissioned officers and 3,656 black female enlisted troops trained at Fort Des Moines represented 4 percent of all WAC troops. A post band kept them hopping throughout the rigorous training. Like the idea of black officers in World War I, the concept of female troops was opposed by much of the

Black WAACs at Fort Des Moines in 1942 avert boredom by playing the piano and singing Negro spirituals and other period tunes. *U.S. Army*

WAACs in formation at Fort Huachuca, Arizona, 1942. *U.S. Army*

The black WAAC band strutted its stuff
with determination at Fort Des Moines
and throughout the surrounding community.
U.S. Army

WAACs marching through downtown Des Moines, Iowa, in 1942 were an unusual but impressive
sight for local citizens. *U.S. Army*

WAC Company B, led by First Lieutenant
Dorothy Scott, Birmingham, England, 1945.
U.S. Army

The popularity of the black WAC/WAAC regimental bands was undeniable, as their music made
the difficult training pass by on a song at Fort Des Moines. *U.S. Army*

World War II military establishment and again dumped at the obscure cavalry post in Iowa for the same reasons.

"The presence of women in the army was resented by many because, traditionally, the military was male. The resentment was doubled by the service of Negro women because the laws, customs, and mores of the World War Two era denigrated the discriminated against Negroes," remembered former

Lieutenant Harriet Ida Pickens and Ensign Frances Mills were the first African-American WAVES to be commissioned, 21 December 1944. *National Archives*

African-American Army women work alongside French civilian personnel at 17th Base Post Office, Paris, France, 1945. *National Archives*

WAC officer Charity Adams Earley. "Negro males had been systematically degraded and mistreated in the civilian world, and the presence of successfully performing Negro women on the scene increased their [whites'] resentment." (Earley 1989)

Led by WAAC director Oveta Culp Hobby, the black and white female troops trained together at Fort Des Moines, but were segregated for dining and housing.

Adams Earley said the first black female officers were as different from each other as night and day, but all were committed to service.

"We [the black female officer candidates] were thirty-nine different personalities, from different family backgrounds and different vocational experiences. . . . We were single, married, divorcees, fiancées. . . . We were the ambitious, the patriotic, the adventurous. We were whomever our environments had made us, and that was what we had to contribute to the WAAC," recalled Adams Earley.

Ours was not an easy life, even with lots of help and too much attention. The first officer candidate class was the guinea pig for the WAAC, and lots of adjustments

continued on page 77

Duchess Arlene

Civilian black women served their country in a variety of capacities that were vitally important to the war effort both inside and outside of the military. Arlene Roberts of Moline, Illinois, for example, possibly saved the life of her future husband, James B. Morris Jr., a year before she met him.

While spending her summer break from the University of Iowa with her brother, Bud, in Chicago in 1945, Roberts applied for a secretarial job at the University of Chicago and was hired at its School of Metallurgy. She was well aware of the war effort through her sweetheart at the time, Tuskegee Airman Lt. Robert Williams, who was flying combat missions over Europe with the 332nd Fighter Group. Williams had named his P-51D Mustang fighter plane the *Duchess Arlene* in her honor.

When Roberts arrived at the School of Metallurgy, due to her speed and accuracy, she was assigned to an elite group of typists working on a top-secret project. On her first day, she met a brilliant black scientist who was leading the project, Dr. Ernest Wilkins Jr. Born in Chicago, Wilkins had enrolled in the University of Chicago at age thirteen, received his bachelor's degree in math at seventeen, his master's degree at eighteen, and his doctorate at nineteen.

After weeks of typing complicated scientific equations on foil, Roberts was assigned to a room by herself to type the final modifications. After the project was finished, staff members were assembled and told that they had prepared the plans for the atomic bomb.

"When they announced that we had been working on the atomic bomb, both scientist and staff members broke down and cried over what this horrible weapon would do,"

"Duchess Arlene" Roberts

she recalled. "We also knew that its use might be necessary to end the war." (Roberts-Morris 1993)

Little did Roberts know that the weapon they created in Chicago might actually have saved the life of her future husband, who was fighting Japanese in the South Pacific. James "Braddie" Morris (see Chapter 6) had broken the color line with his service in the 6th Army "Alamo Force," and the elite unit had already been selected to be the first army infantry regiment to invade mainland Japan. Army intelligence was predicting 1 million American casualties in a mainland invasion, and the chance of Morris, a forward scout, being one of them was extremely high. On 6 August 1945, an enriched-uranium nuclear bomb named Little Boy was dropped on Hiroshima, Japan, killing 140,000 people. A second plutonium-core nuclear bomb, named Fat Man, was dropped on Nagasaki three days later, killing 80,000 and forcing a Japanese surrender, thus canceling the need for the planned 6th Army mainland invasion. World War II was over.

Robert Williams moved to Hollywood, California, after the war and, as an actor and screenwriter, eventually penned the manuscript that would be the basis for the 1995 HBO feature *The Tuskegee Airmen*. In the movie, he was portrayed by actor Laurence Fishburne. His *Duchess Arlene* P-51D was on loan to Airman Lt. Robert Martin when it was shot down over Yugoslavia in March 1945.

Arlene Roberts and James B. Morris Jr. would meet on the University of Iowa campus in 1946 and marry the

Captain Robert W. Williams of the 332nd Fighter Group, 100th Fighter Squadron, flew fifty combat missions over Europe in 1944 and 1945.

Captain Williams on the wing of his *Duchess Arlene* P-51D Mustang fighter plane, in Italy, 1945.

following year. Their three sons would include the author of this book, born in 1958.

Black women contributed to the war effort in many ways—from serving in the WAAC and as nurses to working in factories and typing the plans for the atomic bomb—and their legacy of patriotism and excellence stands beside that of others.

Arlene Roberts met Capt. James "Brad" Morris, shown here during the war, met on the University of Iowa campus in 1946 and were married in 1947.

Captain Williams and Arlene Roberts on a stroll in Chicago, 1945.

Borrowed from Williams by Lt. Robert L. Martin, the *Duchess Arlene* crashed in Yugoslavia in March 1945, on Martin's forty-eighth combat mission. Martin was rescued by Yugoslavian leader Marshal Tito's underground and returned to his unit five weeks later without the airplane. A fiberglass reproduction of the *Duchess Arlene* currently stands as the World War II Iowa Tuskegee Airmen Memorial at the Iowa Air National Guard, 132nd Fighter Wing, Des Moines International Airport, Iowa, founded by the author in 2002.

continued from page 73

had to be made on both sides, by the trainees and the trainers. We were subjected to hundreds of changes during that first six weeks. We were the people upon whom the rules and policies were tried out, changed and tried, and in many cases changed back to the first position. We were the people, as Colonel Hobby said, and said so well, beginning the tradition of women in the service. There were many unpleasant moments and disillusioning experiences, and there were pleasant and hopeful ones. (Earley 1989)

According to official history, the WAC was successful because its mission, to aid the United States in a time of war, was part of a larger national effort that required selfless sacrifice from all Americans. The war effort initiated vast economic and social changes and indelibly altered the role of women in American society. (Bellafaire 1994)

Segregated USO Club, New York City, 1945. *National Archives*

A soldier and a WAC on a walk in Europe, 26 May 1945. *U.S. Army*

CHAPTER 5

World War II: Tuskegee Airmen Soaring Above, 758th Tankers Rumbling Below

Tuskegee Airmen deployed in the 15th Air Force (Army Air Forces), Italy, 21 August 1944. *National Archives*

Tuskegee Airmen Soaring Above

Born in a World War II climate of racial discrimination and degradation, the all-black 332nd Fighter Group, consisting of the 99th, 100th, 301st, and 302nd fighter squadrons, flew 200 bomber-escort missions over Europe without losing an American bomber. The 332nd flew 311 missions with the 15th Air Force, including one that bombed a Daimler-Benz tank-assembly plant in Berlin on 24 March 1945, where it bagged three elite German ME-262 jet fighters. Flying B-17 and B-24 heavy bombers, the entire 15th Air Force dropped 303,842 tons of bombs on twelve countries in Europe and crippled Nazi fuel and aircraft production. It lost 3,364 aircraft, including 21,671 bomber crewman and fighter pilots killed, wounded, or captured.

Captain Luther H. Smith

Of the 992 Tuskegee airmen who served during World War II in Europe, 66 pilots were killed in action and 32 were captured by the Nazis as they destroyed 409 enemy aircraft on 1,578 combat missions. Of their 32 prisoners-of-war, the one with most compelling tale of suffering, determination, and success was Capt. Luther Smith of Des Moines, Iowa, who completed class 43-E at Tuskegee. On 13 October 1944, while returning from the last of 133 combat missions,

Luther H. Smith addresses a huge crowd at Fort Des Moines on dedication weekend, 3 November 2002. Both Joseph Gomer and former POW Smith were in the first Tuskegee Airmen class (1943), and Iowa had the distinction of having twelve Tuskegee Airmen.

Smith spotted a German railyard with a munitions trains passing through it and decided to attack.

Smith's gunfire ignited the train, which exploded into a huge fireball. He was flying too fast to avoid to the flames and was forced to fly through them. His P-51 caught on fire. As he attempted to gain altitude, he saw that the fire was out of control and rolled the plane so he could bail out.

Unfortunately, as he exited, his foot was caught, and the impact busted his pelvis in half, turning his entire leg backward. He lost consciousness. He awoke in a head-first free fall, seeing his tattered parachute dragging behind him and that his plane had already passed him in the air and crashed to the ground as a

Captain Luther H. Smith with fellow flight trainees Joseph Gomer, Maurice "Smokey" Esters, and John Briggs graduated with the first class of Tuskegee airmen at Tuskegee Airfield, Alabama, in 1943 and served in the 301st Fighter Squadron in Italy from 1943 to 1944. Esters was later killed when his plane crashed into the Adriatic Sea. Gomer flew 68 missions, and Smith flew 133 missions. *Smith Collection*

Captain Luther H. Smith's P-51B Mustang fighter wore number 93 and was destroyed in his fiery crash in 1944. *Smith Collection*

fireball. He landed in a tree, shattering more of his broken body. The first German troops to arrive at his location climbed the tree and proceeded to rob him. They were prepared to cut off his fingers to get his class ring. Fortunately, a Nazi officer arrived, and he, appreciating the trade value of an American officer, pulled his weapon and ordered the soldiers to stop. They then pulled Smith from the tree and threw him over a horse for transport to a hospital.

Smith spent the next seven months in a Nazi hospital, where the German doctors poorly repaired his broken pelvis and hip and placed him in a full-body plaster cast with maggots inside the wrappings to eat the dead tissue. Refusing to lose his spirit, Smith spent his nights suffering in the dark and his days playing cards with wounded Nazi officers. He even taught himself the German language.

At war's end, Smith was rescued, returned stateside, and endured two more years of operations and therapy, after which his shattered leg was now six inches shorter than it had been. After his semirecovery, he returned to the University of

Iowa to finish his mechanical-engineering degree in 1950 and eventually found employment with General Electric in Pennsylvania, where he became the first black engineer in the NASA aerospace program.

Winner of the Distinguished Flying Cross, the Air Medal with six oak-leaf clusters, and the Purple Heart, Smith became one of seven veterans to accompany President William Clinton to Europe for the fiftieth anniversary of World War II in 1995. He also received the Presidential Gold Medal from President George W. Bush in 2007 and was an inauguration guest of President Barack Obama in 2009.

Captain Smith, recovering from massive injuries, corrective surgeries, and nine months as a Nazi POW, still looked good in 1946. *Smith Collection*

Smith described his war experience in his keynote address at the World War II Iowa Tuskegee Airmen Memorial, Iowa Air National Guard (IANG) 132nd Fighter Wing, on 2 November 2002:

In the 1920s and 1930s, this country was much different than it is today. It was impossible to fly with the U.S Army Air Corps . . . [T]here had been black aviators prior to World War II, but there was no history that blacks could fly and maintain sophisticated military equipment.

When young blacks tried to become military aviators, each of us were told that there was no place for us, and, even if so, there is no military organization that would accept us. But black organizations like the NAACP kept the pressure on.

Early in 1941, a Howard University–educated engineer named Yancey Williams was a licensed, but rejected pilot that pressed his case, and the NAACP pushed to the Supreme Court. A day after the case was filed, the War Department and the U.S. Army Air Corps announced a training facility for black aviators at Tuskegee, Alabama, in 1941.

The first black class of five pilots graduated in March of 1943, leading a total of 992, of which 450 would see combat overseas with the 99th Pursuit Squadron and 100th, 301st, and 302nd fighter squadrons.

It was the opportunity of a lifetime to receive the letter requesting you report to Tuskegee, Alabama, for military aviator training. Each of us had the feeling we would make it, although many were washed out due to a quota system. The Air Corps did not want us, and we felt a bond closer than family. We felt a confidence and determination that helped us succeed when many thought we would fail.

Our first mission over North Africa on June 1, 1943, as the 99th Pursuit Squadron was uneventful. But Charles Hall of Indiana became the first airman to shoot down an enemy [Nazi German] aircraft while some white commanders were requesting that our unit be dissolved and our equipment given to white squadrons. Our black commander, Col. Benjamin O. Davis, was ordered to testify on our behalf in Washington, D.C., and supreme commander Gen. George Marshall backed him up in our support.

Our second mission was Italy with the 15th Air Force, with our task to assure that the bombers reach their strategic target and return home safely. Col. Davis and his predecessor, Sparky Roberts, realized that we had an advantage with four squadrons [sixty-four airplanes] over the usual three squadrons [forty-eight airplanes], allowing us to fly on both sides, above and behind our bombers. German fighter aircraft would see our numbers and fly on to easier targets.

When the war ended we had made a difference. To this day, veterans of World War II bomber crews come up and thank me for saving their lives and making their dangerous jobs easier.

Many historians believe that our [Tuskegee airmen] success was the beginning of racial integration in America.

Lieutenant Joseph P. Gomer

Born July 20, 1920, in Iowa Falls, Iowa, Joseph P. Gomer would join the first Midwestern class arriving at Tuskegee Institute, Alabama, in September of 1942. He shared his experiences in a personal interview in November 2009, beginning with how he, a graduate of the Civilian Pilot Program in 1940, joined fellow black Iowans Oscar Glass, Maurice Esters, and Luther Smith on a long train ride to Alabama.

"Someone at Ellsworth Junior College had asked me if I wanted to fly and I said, 'OK, I'll try it,' " recalled Gomer.

Joseph P. Gomer tells his personal story on dedication weekend of the World War II Iowa Tuskegee Airmen Memorial at the Iowa National Guard, 132nd Fighter Wing, in Des Moines, Iowa, 3 November 2002.

He had enlisted in the U.S. Army at Fort Leavenworth, Kansas, and was told to go home with no uniform, as they had no place to put him. While there, he heard about the Tuskegee opportunity and applied for aviation-cadet training, eventually receiving orders to report to Alabama in September.

When the black trainees arose for breakfast the first morning on the southbound train, they were directed to the end of the car by the conductor, who pulled a curtain around them. "That was my first taste of racial discrimination," said Gomer. "We pulled the curtain aside, and the conductor pulled it back, and we stormed back to our Pullman car, where we took the rest of our meals."

The truck ride from the railhead to Tuskegee Institute illustrated the black poverty of Alabama. The trainees saw mule-drawn wagons with shoeless, barely clad black children running alongside.

Their training consisted of primary, basic, and advanced levels, under a white commander.

"We flew Stearman biplanes at Moton Field, which was no big deal, and then twenty hours of combat aircraft training in a P-40 single-seat fighter at Tuskegee Airfield, where we were asked to read the tech manual, taxi, and fly," recalled Gomer. "I liked the P-40 and was one hot pilot until, practicing near Auburn, I went into a scary spin from a loop and tried to bail out. When I turned the controls loose, the plane corrected itself, and I was saved."

Commissioned a second lieutenant and assigned to the 301st Fighter Squadron of the 332nd Fighter Group, under command of black Col. Benjamin O. Davis, at Selfridge Field near Detroit, Michigan, the country boy from Iowa experienced urban nightlife, although an eventual race riot led to base confinement.

"We [blacks] had our own officers club and could not go to the white officers club, but did our partying in Detroit anyway," said Gomer. "Detroit was one jumping town!"

The 301st shipped overseas as a P-39 outfit and deployed in early 1944. It took the slow liberty-ship convoy twenty-nine days to enter the Mediterranean Sea and land at Salerno, on the west coast of Italy, where the airmen lived in cold pup tents and ate British "bully beef."

"We flew dawn and dusk missions because we had a lighted airstrip and harbor and convoy patrol with strafing from time to time, with the objective of keeping German aircraft away," he said. "After the Mount Vesuvius volcano erupted in March, we would take off through ash to see a beautiful sunrise over the Mediterranean. We had total air superiority, and our ships were as far as you could see."

We were fighting two battles. I flew for my parents, for my race, for our battle for first-class citizenship and for my country. We were there to break down barriers, open a few doors, and do a job. But we're all Americans. That's why we chose to fight. I'm as American as anybody. My black ancestors were brought over here, perhaps against their will, to help build America. My German ancestors came over to build a new life and my Cherokee ancestors were here to greet all the boats.

We [the 301st] were committed to fighting for our country although we served in a segregated air unit. In reality, the black tankers and infantry surviving the bloodbath on the ground in Italy were the real heroes.

—Lt. Joseph P. Gomer

Finally, Colonel Davis alerted his flyers to a new mission: bomber escort for the 15th Air Force. "Our enthusiasm was blunted with our assignment to old P-47 Thunderbolts while the white groups were getting the elite P-51 Mustang," Gomer recalled. After only fifteen missions in the slow, but heavily armed (with eight 50-caliber machine guns) P-47s, the 301st received P-51C aircraft, and its pilots were elated.

But casualties were mounting. One particular bomber-escort mission went terribly bad for the 301st when bad weather affected its ability to find the B17s on their way to Germany, resulting in fifteen bombers, with 1,500 crewmen, blown from the sky.

Brigadier General Benjamin O. Davis Sr., the father of the Tuskegee Airmen's commander, on an inspection tour of Europe, 1944. *U.S. Army*

Members of the 332nd Fighter Group attending a briefing in Ramitelli, Italy, March 1945: (left to right) Robert W. Williams, Ottumwa, Iowa; William H. Holloman, St. Louis, Missouri; Ronald W. Reeves, Washington, D.C.; Christopher W. Newman, St. Louis; Walter M. Downs, New Orleans, Louisiana. *Library of Congress*

"Myself and my wingman, Eugene Brown, were one of only four of our P-51s to find the bombers and were quickly jumped by twelve ME109s, who were above us. And as soon as we broke the cloud bank, they attacked. We dove in and broke them up, and Brown exited a cloud to find himself flying between two ME109s," recalled Gomer. "He proceeded to shoot down three enemy fighters before being blown from the sky and becoming a Nazi POW for the remainder of the war. Our failure to show up in force cost fifteen bombers that day."

Another potentially deadly obstacle confronting the black airmen in Italy was indifference and slight by the white fighter pilots, who were veteran flyers with valuable experience.

Captain Virgil Dixon stands by an M-5 Stewart tank of the 758th Tank Battalion in Italy 1944.

Lieutenant Colonel Benjamin O. Davis, Jr. commander of the Tuskegee Airmen, 1944. He was the son of Brig. Gen. Benjamin O. Davis Sr. *U.S. Air Force*

"The white fighter groups who had been flying the P-51s refused to brief us on their experiences, so we were trial by error, and the death toll rose," said Gomer. "By the fall of 1944, I had lost all my tent mates and was living alone. Airmen Faulkner, Maples, Williams, and Valentine were all lost on missions. I knew that after sixty-eight missions, if I kept flying, something was going to happen."

Gomer requested rotation and received orders on Christmas Day, 1944. Preparing to return stateside, he stood in line with other officers to board the SS *America*, facing the most humiliating moment of his war experience.

"When it came my time to board, a fat, short redneck sergeant put an N by my name and ordered me to the back of the line as the white officers watched in silence," Gomer painfully recalled. "Even the white enlisted men boarded before

Captain Dixon (far left) discusses directions with a tank crew of the 758th Tank Battalion in Italy 1945: "Here's where we're going."

Captain Dixon stands before tent city at Livorno (Leghorn), Italy, on 11 December 1945: "Tent City, I ain't mad, Ha, Ha."

Black soldiers of the 758th Tank Battalion, attached to the 92nd Division, parade before the citizens in Naples, Italy, in 1945. The 92nd suffered 5,000 casualties in the Italian campaign against stiff Nazi resistance.

me. Had I felt about the Germans the way I did about that redneck sergeant, the war would have been over much faster."

Returning stateside brought no satisfaction for the black airmen. "We came back as black combat veterans, not heroes," said Gomer, who would remain in the service and fly in the Korean War. "German POWs had more rights than we [blacks] did as we returned to the same old racial discrimination."

A half century and many recent accolades later, the surviving white pilots of the 359th Heavy Bomb Group were holding a reunion in Saint Paul, Minnesota, and invited Tuskegee airman Gomer to attend.

"Several bomber pilots approached me with tears in their eyes and said, 'We have waited fifty years to thank you guys for saving our asses,' " recalled Gomer. "I guess they [whites] really did appreciate our efforts."

La Verna Oliphant: The Silent Front

La Verna Oliphant arrived at the Tuskegee Institute in 1943 as the new wife of Cadet Clarence Oliphant, who would fly fifty combat missions with the 99th Pursuit Squadron and the 302nd Fighter Squadron, 332nd Fighter Group, against Nazi Germany. Lieutenant Oliphant named his P-51 Mustang fighter La Verna *in his wife's honor.*

La Verna Oliphant during World War II. She was a featured speaker at the Iowa Tuskegee Airmen Memorial ceremony in November 2002. *La Verna Oliphant*

Our names will not be listed or recorded anywhere, but nothing can take away the beauty of seeing it all take place before our eyes and the sharing of the Tuskegee experience.

The bond was there, and in essence we were like an auxiliary, but unformed and unorganized, and knowing that this was the way it would remain. Our purpose, encouragement and support for this new venture that this select group would encounter to make them a first in history—namely, the Tuskegee airmen.

Jessie Morris, Claudine Winston, and myself, La Verna Oliphant, were there in Tuskegee during some great portions of these times. There were others, of course, and I cannot begin to list all who participated in this wonderful experience.

For some of us, it really reached the heights of new experiences and changes in lifestyles, reached explosive stages that were unknown to us in the early 1940s. Segregation and inequities of social justices were more than just studies in Negro history or spoken words of wisdom from our elders. New elements of living and appreciation for fortitude were introduced in a different perspective than ever before, but it all led to development for us and proved to be an experience that could almost parallel the training of the cadets.

The feeling of having been a part of it—being surrounded by it, as we were through the years 1943 to 1945—still brings vivid memories that are treasured as being a part of history. We were there to watch the cadets march and sing and were aware of many of the activities that were a part of the routine. We became acquainted with the history and glory of the famed Tuskegee Institute and were able to roam the campus to observe its prestige.

We witnessed despair and worry when some were having trouble with some phase of the training, and we tried to help them if we could. We knew who was flying on certain days and prayed for their safe return. We cried when they didn't make it back. We watched the ones who made it to graduation day and felt the same pride for each, whether he was known to us or not.

Some of us continued from graduation to the bases where the airmen were assigned before departure for overseas duties. All too many waited for word of safe return or other knowledge of the pilots' whereabouts as each performed on their respective flight missions. All accomplishments had meaning for us all.

The ranks and files of those who are still with it from the beginning to the present day are very likely diminished in a proportion similar to the Tuskegee airmen. But no matter what the year of entry into the ranks of the silent front, we all have the bond of the total experience. (Oliphant 1984)

Cadet Clarence A. Oliphant of the 99th Pursuit Squadron. Oliphant gained fame for mistakenly joining a white P-38 squadron for a raid on "Hitler's Hideaway" in 1944. "When the formation of P-38s, plus the P-51, reached the target in Southeastern, Austria, Lt. Oliphant was determined to contribute something toward the success of the mission," said *Courier* war correspondent Collins George from Italy. "As the P-38s released their bombs, Oliphant put his aircraft into a dive and released both wing tanks over the target area."

First Lieutenant Clarence A. Oliphant, Italy, 1944.

Captain Russell L. Collins of Davenport, Iowa, one of the last surviving Tuskegee Airmen, trained at Tuskegee as a flight officer.
Photo courtesy of African American Museum of Iowa

To the officers and men of the 92nd Division, who have trained and fought so well, I extend my unfounded admiration and sincere thanks for duty well performed.

—Maj. Gen. E. M. Almond,

Commander, 92nd Division, 758th

Tank Battalion, Italy, 1945

758th Tankers Rumbling Below

As the Tuskegee airmen soared above, the black tankers of the 758th Tank Battalion rumbled below against a rear-guard action by brilliant German field marshal Albert Kesselring.

The 758th Tank Battalion, 5th Tank Group, was formed at Fort Knox, Kentucky, in 1941 with the motto "We Pierce" on their M-5 tanks. Named Tuskers, the unit included the future first black professional baseball player, Jackie Robinson, who had been transferred from the 761st after a racial incident on a civilian bus. The 758th was attached first to the 5th Army and then to the all-black 92nd Division (formed during World War I), and it was led by a second generation of black officers, including Lt. Virgil F. Dixon, who described the best and worst of tank war in Italy. Dixon, who was born in 1916, served with the U.S. Army 758th Tank Regiment, attached to the 92nd Infantry Division, in Italy from 1943 to 1945. He later graduated Drake University Law School and became a prominent attorney and political figure in Chicago, Illinois, after the war. His testimony is from an interview with the author in July 1992. He passed away in 1993. His widow, Nathaline Lewis-Dixon, is an Iowa native and historian.

"We were moving forward at dusk one day, and the German 88mm guns were firing from high ground so far away that we could not see them. The German spotters were so good that they hit our first three moving tanks dead center, destroying them and killing their crews as we pulled back. As dark came, we knew the German sappers would wire the dead tanks with explosives, attempting to kill our recovery crews as well," recalled Dixon.

The black junior officers of the 758th often questioned commands from senior white officers, who sometimes appeared indifferent to and even contentious because of their duty commanding black troops. Dixon continued, "Although our white captain was aware of the common German trick and that they had had time to set booby traps through the night, he ordered our recovery crews forward at dawn. The first tank they opened exploded, killing six black soldiers who should have lived to fight another day and see their loved ones again. The incident haunts me to this day and reminds me of the war against allied racism we fought under Nazi gunfire."

The 92nd Division, with the attached 758th tankers, suffered over 5,000 casualties during the Italian campaign against ferocious German resistance. The campaign ended in a stalemate.

Captain Virgil F. Dixon of the 758th Tank Battalion, Italy, 1945. Dixon's M-5 tanks were easy prey for the German 88mm antitank guns firing from higher ground.

M-5 Stewart tanks of the 758th Tank Battalion, attached to the 92nd Division, celebrate victory over the Germans with a parade in Naples, Italy, in 1945.

CHAPTER 6

World War II:
Song of the South Pacific

This World War II poster, "United We Win," features integrated aircraft factory workers.

THEIR THEME SONG was one of pain and degradation, and the bitter taste of racial segregation was a daily meal for black soldiers serving in the South Pacific during World War II. In spite of the tremendous barriers facing black soldiers fighting Imperial Japan, there were small breaks through the color line.

James Brad Morris Jr. had followed his World War I black-officer father and, with an army scholarship, enlisted after graduating the University of Iowa in 1941, where he had also participated in reserve officers' training corps (ROTC).

"In the thirties, Negroes avoided ROTC, because in the white schools, they were refused the right to qualify for a commission. Brad was the exception," according to Morris's Kappa Alpha Psi fraternity brother Sterling Dover in 1997. "He eagerly took the 'Basic ROTC,' and built on it for the future. He loved it! We

Private First Class James B. Morris Jr. shoots a rifle during basic training at Fort Leonard Wood, Missouri, in 1941. "After going through that [basic training], I can truthfully say that I am a real soldier and a man. . . . It was a fine experience and showed what the boys are made of," Morris wrote in a letter to his family.

When bombs are dropping all around you and the ground pitches and tosses like a wild sea, there are no atheists. They say there are no atheists in a foxhole and believe you me, it's the truth. There are no social barriers or color lines in one either. Everyone gets in there together and prays to God that they don't drop one in your midst.

—Lt. James B. Morris Jr.
6th Army "Alamo Force,"
from a 1944 letter home

loved him, but we thought he was crazy. But he kept the rest of us brothers in laughing 'stitches' with his loud boasts: 'I'm the god-dag number-one man in the god-dag first platoon!' Of course, Braddie had an advantage that the rest of us lacked—namely, the inspiring example of a father who had served in the First World War as a commissioned officer. Nevertheless, it took a lot of faith, determination, and persistence to accomplish what Braddie did."

After attending a civilian military training corps (CMTC) camp at Fort Riley, Kansas, in 1936 and ROTC during college, Morris was on a military roll. Morris's basic training with Company D, 34th Engineering Training Battalion, at Fort Leonard Wood, Missouri, was interrupted by the Japanese attack at Pearl Harbor, Hawaii, on 7 December, 1941, prompting his immediate transfer to army intelligence headquarters in Washington, D.C., and then a transfer to South Pacific headquarters in Sydney, Australia, in early 1942.

As a special agent investigator, Morris ran top-secret correspondence and performed undercover assignments for the Special Service Section in Australia and stateside. In the United States, he posed as a civilian employee, a welfare worker, attempting to expose the Japanese Black Dragon Society's efforts to recruit disgruntled black factory workers in Detroit, Michigan, for sabotage operations during the summer of 1942.

"After I left school, I never heard from Braddie until I bumped into [him] in Detroit and recognized him although dressed as a civilian," recalled Dover. "Apparently, Braddie was 'undercover,' checking the possibility that the Japanese Black Dragon Society was attempting to subvert Negro defense workers."

After returning to Australia, Morris entered officer-candidate school (OCS) at Camp Columbia, Brisbane, Australia, on 2 April 1943, graduating at the top of his 700-member class on 11 June 1943 and drawing the attention of the national black media. Morris was horrified when he was assigned to a racially segregated transportation unit at headquarters Base B along with his other black classmates, who had all come from transportation units. He wrote to his commanding general on 24 January 1944: "Prior to going to OCS, I was assigned a special agent investigator in the office of the A.C. of S., G-2. . . . All my commissioned service has been with G-2 and I have never been assigned to a transportation unit nor have I performed any transportation duty. . . . I feel that my service would be more valuable as an infantry officer in military intelligence."

Morris had also been noticed by new 6th Army commander, Lt. Gen. Walter Krueger, who would eventually assign Morris to his I Corps intelligence detail. The unit had the legendary code name "Alamo Force," to avoid operational control by Australian generals. The unit's motto was "Born of War." (The legendary Alamo Force would become the predecessor of today's army Special Forces.) After escaping the racially segregated transportation company via relentless requests for transfer based on his pre-OCS intelligence work for the Special Service Section, Morris was finally reassigned to 6th Army intelligence on 30 January 1944, after receiving orders from Lt. Col. W. A. Olson. His unprecedented assignment to this unit broke the rigid racial color line.

"I am the only Negro officer in this base headquarters, but that makes no difference to me . . . ," Morris wrote in a letter home. "This only serves as a challenge to my ability, integrity and initiative."

His new assignment would land him in heavy combat in New Guinea and later the Central Philippines, where he would win the Bronze Star between 1944 and 1945. Morris served in a racially integrated intelligence unit and commanded white troops in combat. However, the overall army was still segregated, and his dining and housing quarters were often separate from those of white troops.

"In the jungles, if you were wounded, you didn't ask whether the man carrying you to safety was white or black. The segregation in Australia was brought on by the Americans," Morris wrote in a letter home. "A puzzled Australian said to me, 'You are an officer, and you are a black Yank?' I said I

Staff Sergeant Morris arrived at U.S. Army's South Pacific headquarters in Sydney, Australia, in 1942. "Those Japs [who participated in the Pearl Harbor attack] certainly had their nerve jumping on us. . . . Now is really the time for all good men to come to the aid of their country," Morris wrote to his family during his basic training.

Sergeant Morris types on an ammo crate while serving the Special Service Section in 1942 in Australia, where he performed investigative work and carried top-secret correspondence prior to his acceptance in officer-candidate school.

Lieutenant Morris shows a Thompson submachine gun on New Guinea in 1944. "We trudged over mountains which were 5,000 feet high and it was really a grueling task. Those natives ran over the hills like deer and almost killed us because we were trying to keep up with them," Morris wrote.

After graduation from officer candidate school atop his 700-member class at Camp Columbia, Brisbane, Australia, Lt. Morris receives his bars from Capt. E. B. Lowe in 1943. News and photographs of Morris's accomplishment appeared in black papers throughout the United States. *National Archives*

was, and he replied, 'But the white yanks have been telling us that there are no colored officers.' "

Activated in January of 1943, the Alamo Force commanded army units involved in *Operation Cartwheel*, which sought to isolate the Japanese base Rabul, in New Britain, by attacking along New Guinea's northeast coast and nearby islands and western New Britain. Specializing in armed landings that would establish garrisons and airfields to support future attacks, the Alamo Force was relieved on New Guinea by the 8th Army in September 1944. Morris described a typical mission on New Guinea in a 27 July 1943 letter to his parents: "We were on patrol one day, reached a native village and found a lone Jap who had been left behind by his buddies. The natives told us that there were twenty of them who came back to the village to sleep each night and steal enough food to keep them alive. We left before dawn so that we could get them before they left in the morning. It was a large patrol so just a few of the men went along. We killed them all, and we all came back OK."

Morris's forward-scouting unit participated in the 20 October 1944 invasion of Leyte, in the Philippines, and then fought at Luzon on 9 January 1945, facing heavy combat all the way. During the long and tedious 6th Army campaign on New Guinea, from 1943 to 1944, Morris and Lt. Joe Clark, who was white, took the brazen move of approaching their commanding officer for a new and more dangerous assignment. On 12 November 1943, they cowrote to their commanding officer, Lt. Col. N. B. Sauve:

> We feel that we can say without being immodest that we have encountered and been able to overcome most difficulties peculiar to operations in a forward area. We therefore feel qualified for further duty in even more advanced areas. . . . We feel that we could work together indefinitely, in complete harmony and with an efficiency that would do credit to us and the Intelligence Service.
>
> We request that, in light of the foregoing remarks, some thought be given to the possibility of using us as a two officer "team" to proceed with task forces sent out for the mission of establishing advanced bases. We feel that such a team could be of great value to G-2.

Alamo Force/6th Army patch

Papuan natives pose with a Japanese rifle and helmet after an ambush on New Guinea in 1944. "The native holding the rifle also wears the belt and the bayonet of the Jap which we had disposed of," Morris wrote. "The little fellow on the left was really comical and he was a good scout. It was a pleasure to watch those fellows go through the jungle and over the hills. . . . They really know their stuff and taught us a lot."

For a black junior officer of an integrated intelligence unit within a racially segregated army to request such a bold assignment was unprecedented. On 26 January 1944, he and Clark again wrote Sauve with a request for more action:

> We feel that 50% of our capabilities are wasted on our present assignment. . . . [T]here is no longer much scope left for originality or initiative. We are young. We have thrived on tropical service. We do not think we have a hero complex, but we are full of vitality and the desire for adventure. . . . We would have a chance to use our initiative and aggressiveness. . . . We think we could perform a service

A Papuan native with leprosy shows broken skin and missing fingers. Disease killed more natives and Allied and enemy troops than war did during the long (1942 to 1945) New Guinea campaign against the entrenched Japanese 18th Army.

Lieutenant Morris poses with a Thompson submachine gun after the October 1944 invasion of Leyte. Japanese bombing on the second day included 200 aircraft and was the largest Japanese antipersonnel air attack in World War II.

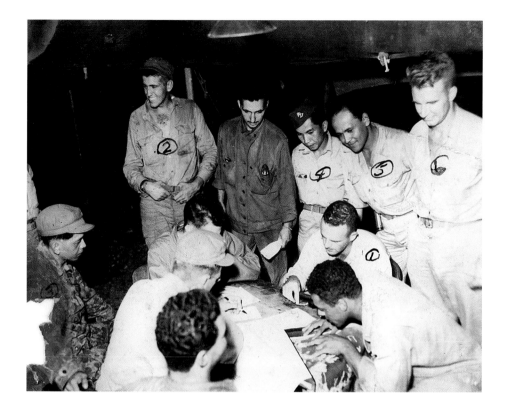

Lieutenant Morris (lower right) reads a map at an officers' briefing before a mission on Luzon in 1945. The racially mixed officer group included Nisei (Japanese-American) and Filipino officers. "I am the only Negro officer in this base so I am really watching my Ps and Qs," Morris said. "I am going to do my best to make them [whites] appreciate me and my ability. . . . I can't let anyone down."

which would be a "feather in the cap" of USSOS Intelligence. We request that we be given roving or liaison assignments which allow us to cover continuously the forward areas of New Britain and New Guinea. We feel that, at very least, this idea is worth being put to a test.

Meanwhile, Morris's superior work continued to be noticed throughout 6th Army command. "It is with extreme pleasure that I hereby commend you for the excellent manner of presentation of the Base 'B' Intelligence Summary for the month of March 1944," wrote Lt. Col. John Schermerhorn on 3 April 1944. "Your Summary could well serve as a working guide for the future rendition of Base Intelligence Summaries."

On 29 April 1944, Morris's work and aggressive requests finally paid off when he became the first black officer assigned as a forward scout, passing through Taylor Beach on his way to Hollandia, Dutch New Guinea, and his first Bronze Star Medal of Valor. He was awarded the medal, "for meritorious conduct in the performance of outstanding service at Hollandia, Dutch New Guinea, from 4 May 1944 to 25 May 1944, in connection with military operations against the enemy," by Brig. Gen. J. L. Holman on 9 January 1945.

World War II

Although no black American troops were honored with the Medal of Honor during World War II, a 1992 study by Shaw University found that "systematic racial discrimination had been present in the criteria for awarding medals during World War II." The Shaw study recommended that several black Distinguished Service Cross awards be upgraded to the Medal of Honor. A half-century later in 1997, President William Clinton awarded the medal to seven black World War II veterans, of which Vernon Baker was the only one still alive.

2nd Lt. Vernon Baker of the 370th Infantry, 92nd Division repeatedly risked his life fighting Germans near Castle Aghinoffi, Italy, 1945. **Staff Sgt. Edward Carter** of the 12th Armored Division was wounded five times, killing six Germans and capturing two near Speyer, Germany, 1945. **Lt. John Fox** of the 366th Infantry, 92nd Division remained atop a house to direct artillery fire and died with one hundred Germans, Sommocolonia, Italy, 1944. **Pfc. Willy James Jr.** of the 413th Infantry Regiment, 104th Division was killed while aiding his platoon leader near Lippoldsberg, Germany, 1945. **Staff Sgt. Ruben Rivers** of the 761st Tank Battalion was killed in tank warfare near Guebling, France, 1944, and **1st Lt. Charles Thomas** of the 614th Tank Destroyer Battalion rescued wounded soldiers while he was severely injured near Climbach, France, 1944. **Pfc. George Watson** of the 29th Quartermaster Regiment drowned attempting to save others after his ship was sunk by enemy bombers in 1943.

Baker image: National Archives;
Carter and Thomas images: Library of Congress

Vernon Baker, congratulated by President Clinton in the East Room of the White House, January 13, 1997.

Edward Carter   Charles Thomas

In addition to locating and killing his Japanese enemies, Morris gained popularity with the native Filipinos, who were often abused by white American troops.

"Boasting a similar complexion to theirs, I quickly became very popular with the Filipino guides who were often insulted and humiliated by the white American soldiers," recalled Morris. "Often, when I questioned Filipinos, they would use an expression which means 'you are good.' As a man would say it, he would touch the back of his hand and then touch mine to indicate the same color."

This portrait of Captain James Morris Jr. who was described as an "alert, enthusiastic and capable officer," illustrates his vigor and determination after his 1945 promotion, while he was on Luzon. Captain Morris served with the elite 6th Army Alamo Force, earning a Bronze Star in the South Pacific between 1944 and 1945. Malaria, the atomic bomb, and Japan's surrender prevented the Alamo Force from becoming the first army regiment to land on mainland Japan, where war planners predicted one million Allied casualties if an invasion were necessary.

UNITED STATES CITIZEN
IDENTITY CARD

JAMES B. MORRIS

is an accredited employee of

UNITED STATES ARMY ~~XXXXXXXXXXXXXXXXXX~~
SERVICES OF SUPPLY, SWPA

~~She~~ (He) is employed at

Special Services Office

and is classified as

Welfare worker

DESCRIPTION

Age 23   Height 5'8½"

Weight 175 lbs

Eye Color Brown   Hair Color Black

Sergeant Morris's undercover "welfare worker" identification was used during his Special Service Section mission in Detroit, Michigan, in 1942. He interviewed black factory workers about contact with the Japanese Black Dragon Society, but found nothing.

On 9 September 1945, Morris was promoted to captain and continued to draw praise from his former commanding officers.

"You know I have always valued your work which in my opinion has been consistently of a superior quality," wrote Lt. Col. James Pros on 11 September 1945. "Of all the young men promoted, you are the most deserving," added Colonel Sauve on 19 September. "It has been a privilege to work with you." According to Col. E. J. Barnette, writing on 14 September, "Your conscientious work has merited this promotion, and is greatly appreciated by me." Morris's 30 June 1945 efficiency report by Capt. H. Weyerstall, Base K, described Morris as "[a]n alert, enthusiastic and capable officer who performs his duties quickly and efficiently," adding, "He is a hard worker of high physical endurance. His personality and manner inspire confidence."

The 6th Army was designated to be the first army ground force to invade mainland Japan, but the atomic bombs and the Japanese surrender made the invasion unnecessary and, along with malaria, ended Morris's military combat experience. After barely surviving the malaria, he returned home weighing less than 100 pounds. He would later learn that the final plans for the atomic bomb were typed by his future wife, "Duchess Arlene" Roberts, whom he would meet on the University of Iowa campus in 1946. (See Chapter 4.)

When President Harry Truman dismissed General Douglas MacArthur, Morris's former commanding officer, as supreme commander in the South Pacific on 11 April 1951, Morris's reaction summarized his disgust with army racial discrimination. He wrote:

> I shed no tears about MacArthur's summary dismissal. . . . My aversion to him stems mainly from the rotten manner he treated Negro troops in the Southwest Pacific area. He not only allowed flagrant discrimination and segregation—in many instances he actually encouraged and engendered it by his refusal/or failure to do anything about terrible situations brought to his attention. My duties as an intelligence officer gave me an excellent opportunity to observe many of these practices in operation. . . . Mac was involved in many of them.

Recreational facilities like this swimming pool for black enlisted men ("separate but equal") were still segregated during this, the summer of 1942. By the end of the war, the official policy began to change, requiring commanders to grant access regardless of race. *U.S. Army*

A black military police detachment at the Tuskegee Army Air Field, 1943. Colonel Noel Parrish, the base commander, insisted that his MPs leave their weapons at the guard room when they patrolled nearby towns to prevent violence by local whites who might be "offended" at the sight of blacks carrying guns. *U.S. Army*

Dorie Miller was famous for his bravery in firing on the enemy with antiaircraft guns— on which he had no prior training—during the Japanese attack on Pearl Harbor. He became the first African American awarded the Navy Cross. *U.S. Army*

The Black Experience in World War II

Stewards and officers from the escort carrier *Copahee*, 1944. Note that the three chief stewards at the center of the second row wear uniforms different from petty officers in other specialties. *National Archives*

Black soldiers of the racially segregated 25th Regimental Combat Team, Bougainville, Solomon Islands, April 1944. *U.S. Army*

Black sailors in 1944 stand by the destroyer escort USS *Mason*, which had a crew composed largely of African-Americans. *National Archives*

William Baldwin, the first black man recruited into the U.S. Navy for general service rather than as a steward, sworn in 2 June 1942. *National Archives*

Sergeant addressing an aviation squadron during inspection, 1943.
U.S. Army

Janitors at a North American Aviation aircraft factory form a "V" for "Victory," 1942. *National Archives*

In February 1944, the U.S. Navy commissioned its first African-American officers. The twelve commissioned officers, and a warrant officer who received his rank at the same time, came to be known as the "Golden Thirteen." (Bottom row, left to right): Ensign James E. Hare; Ensign Samuel E. Barnes; Ensign George C. Cooper; Ensign William S. White; Ensign Dennis D. Nelson; (middle row, left to right): Ensign Graham E. Martin; Warrant Officer Charles B. Lear; Ensign Phillip G. Barnes; Ensign Reginald E. Goodwin; (top row, left to right): Ensign John W. Reagan; Ensign Jesse W. Arbor; Ensign Dalton L. Baugh; Ensign Frank E. Sublett. *U.S. Navy*

Black sailors training at the Great Lakes
Naval Training Center, September 1942.
National Archives

Engineer construction troops, Liberia, July 1942. *U.S. Army*

Pilots of the 332nd Fighter Group, briefed for
a combat mission in Italy. *U.S. Army*

Black troops of the 93rd Division engage in trench warfare in the South Pacific, 1943. *U.S. Army*

A gun crew of Battery B, 598th Field Artillery, moves into position near the Arno River, Italy, September 1944. *U.S. Army*

Troops of the 93rd Division packing mortar shells cross the "West Branch Texas River" in Bougainville, Solomon Islands, April 1944. *U.S. Army*

The Fort Huachuca, Arizona, service club. *U.S. Army*

Messmen who volunteered as gunners in a
Pacific task force, July 1942. *U.S. Army*

Seabees attend to an undermined water tank
in the South Pacific, 1942. *U.S. Army*

Labor battalion troops pause for a hot meal at Massacre Bay, Aleutian Islands, May 1943.
U.S. Army

Support troops participate in the landing of the 1st Marine Division on Peleliu, 15 September, 1944. *U.S. Army*

Medical attendants take a well-deserved rest, Peleliu, October 1944. *U.S. Army*

Specialists repair aircraft at the Naval Air Station, Seattle, Washington, 1945. *U.S. Army*

The 22nd Special Construction Battalion celebrates V-J day, 14 August 1945. *U.S. Army*

CHAPTER 7

Korea and Vietnam:
Combat Integration and Black Power

A black gun crew of the 2nd Infantry Division, Korea, 21 May 1951. Segregated and integrated units coexisted in the early years of integration in the military to allow comparative evaluations, which found that the integration of black soldiers into white combat units had been accomplished "without undue friction and with the better utilization of manpower," according to the studies. *National Archives*

The Korean War, 1950–1952

President Harry Truman's 1948 executive order ending racial segregation in the military was ignored by military commanders, and the last segregated unit, the 24th Infantry (founded 1869) was not disbanded until the Korean War in October 1951. Black troops constituted 8 percent of the total U.S. military presence, comprising 9.7 percent of the army, 4.4 percent of the air force, and 3 percent of navy forces and being mixed into all combat units in Korea.

Of the 600,000 black troops that served valiantly during the Korean War, over 5,000 were killed in action at obscure places like Yech'on and the Chosin Reservoir, fighting North Korean and Chinese forces, as well as blistering cold in the winter, sweltering heat in the summer, bugs, parasites, and diseases.

Black Korean War heroes, like infantry commander Lt. Col. Samuel Pierce Jr., led the recapture of Yech'on, where Capt. Charles Bussey killed fifty enemy soldiers. The twenty-five black U.S. Air Force pilots in 1950 included Capt. Daniel "Chappie" James Jr., who flew 101 dangerous missions in his F-86 Sabre jet and navy flier ensign Jesse Brown, who died providing ground support to the 7th Marines at the breakout from Chosin Reservoir in January 1950.

Black U.S. Army, 9th Infantry, soldiers evacuate wounded from Hill 201 in Korea, 19 September 1950. *National Archives*

Even in the face of evidence to the contrary, some people consciously and willingly hold onto racist and prejudicial viewpoints. . . . Properly trained, the American soldier is unmatched, no matter what his race or background. There is no substitute for preparedness."

—Lt. Gen. Julius W. Becton Jr.,
    *Becton: A Soldier
    and Public Servant*

Sergeant George W. Johnson (photo taken in 1950) was a combat medic in Korea, where he treated more casualties from allied friendly artillery fire than enemy bullets. *Johnson Collection*

Black 9th Infantry soldiers assist in evacuating wounded from Hill 201, Korea, 1950. *National Archives*

Korea: A Medic in Harms Way

For combat medic and NCO George Warren Johnson, saving American, South and North Korean, and Chinese lives in the midst of battle was a challenge no matter what color you were. Born in Marshalltown, Iowa, in 1927, Johnson had attended college before being drafted and inducted at Fort Knox, Kentucky, and going through racially segregated basic training at Fort Lee, Virginia.

Sergeant Johnson embarked westward from the Port of Chicago, California—site of the World War II racial incident—and arrived at Inchon Harbor, Korea, in late 1950, where his unit waded ashore along a rope. Due to his high I.Q. and specialty rating, Johnson was made a combat medic. He had no prior medic training. "I was told to learn from the white medics, who had been trained at Fort Sam Houston, Texas, and on the job, if I lived that long," he said. (Johnson 2008)

Johnson was assigned to the U.S. Army 3rd Battalion, 24th Division, 21st Regiment, M Company, which was a heavy-weapons unit providing overhead fire for infantry units digging out the enemy. Although he was in combat and under enemy fire immediately, the greatest danger was from allied artillery fired short. The American medics carried weapons and did not wear red crosses on their arms, as it made them a great target for snipers.

"The rifle companies digging out the enemy got slaughtered, and I was buried in blood and guts from day one," recalled Johnson. In addition to American and NATO troops, Johnson treated South and North Koreans and later Chinese troops, and his success often made the difference between life and death and sometimes meant surrender.

"Our planes dropped leaflets encouraging the enemy troops to surrender, as they were cold and starving and would surrender in droves. One day the two entrenched sides ceased fire when I was called up the hill to treat a wounded North Korean officer. The enemy were poorly equipped and mostly old men and skinny boys, and this officer was shorter than me and couldn't have weighed eighty pounds," recalled Johnson. "With a hundred rifles pointed at me, I treated his arm and gave him a cigarette so his comrades could see he was being treated fairly. They then hoisted a white flag and surrendered."

The Chinese entrance into the war was not a surprise to the South Korean troops, who had been warning the Americans of Chinese infiltration for weeks.

"The South Korean allied soldiers had been warning us about Chinese spies by saying 'China-Boy' to American troops, who ignored their words and seemed surprised by the Chinese onslaught. One day in combat, I looked around to be surrounded by black infantry, and I knew the brothers had arrived big time," said Johnson.

After Johnson's initial prep in the field, the wounded would be carried away from the front line on a litter by South Korean troops, who would sometimes get scared and run leaving the wounded Americans rolling down the hills. If the wounded made it to the battalion aid station, they had a 50 percent chance of survival and would receive a helicopter or ambulance ride to a regimental hospital like the one featured in the movie and TV series *M*A*S*H*. The four-season Korean weather was to Johnson's liking, as it was the same as that of his native Iowa; both areas were on the 38th Parallel.

Johnson survived the Korean War and returned to the United States to Wayne State University, in Nebraska, becoming the first black graduate in 1957 and later becoming an art teacher at Benson High School in Omaha.

"Serving with troops under fire in combat, I tried but could not save many who died, and I carry that with me to this day," said Johnson. "I knew many of them personally and grieve for them like family."

With the civil-rights movement raging at home, the bravery and sacrifices made by black servicemen and women during the Korean War set the stage for the next American conflict in Southeast Asia a decade later.

It was horrible to see young people maimed and crippled for life and I was so busy saving men that the thought never hit me that I could be killed myself.

—Sgt. George W. Johnson, 1950

Integration of the Armed Forces, 1948–1963

A historic document, Executive Order 9981, was signed by President Harry Truman in 1948:

> Establishing the President's Committee on Equality of Treatment and Opportunity in the Armed Forces.
>
> WHEREAS it is essential that there be maintained in the armed services of the United States the highest standards of democracy, with equality of treatment and opportunity for all those who serve in our country's defense:
>
> NOW THEREFORE, by virtue of the authority vested in me as President of the United States, by the Constitution and the statutes of the United States, and as Commander in Chief of the armed services, it is hereby ordered as follows:
>
> 1. It is hereby declared to be the policy of the President that there shall be equality of treatment and opportunity for all persons in the armed services without regard to race, color, religion or national origin. This policy shall be put into effect as rapidly as possible, having due regard to the time required to effectuate any necessary changes without impairing efficiency or morale.
>
> 2. There shall be created in the National Military Establishment an advisory committee to be known as the President's Committee on Equality of Treatment and Opportunity in the Armed Services, which shall be composed of seven members to be designated by the President.
>
> 3. The Committee is authorized on behalf of the President to examine into the rules, procedures and practices of the Armed Services in order to determine in what respect such rules, procedures and practices

"The Return of the Soldier" by Charles White, 1946. This drawing depicts a policeman backed by a klansman holding a whip, pointing his gun at three African-American soldiers returning home following World War II. *Library of Congress*

> may be altered or improved with a view to carrying out the policy of this order. The Committee shall confer and advise the Secretary of Defense, the Secretary of the Army, the Secretary of the Navy, and the Secretary of the Air Force, and shall make such recommendations to the President and to said Secretaries as in the judgment of the Committee will effectuate the policy hereof.

President Truman meets with government officials and committee members who played key roles in the implementation of military desegregation: Seated with the president, left to right: James Forrestal, Secretary of Defense, and influential Connecticut industrialist Alphonsus J. Donahue. Standing, left to right: Thomas R. Reid, Chairman of the Department of Defense Personnel Policy Board; Brig. Gen. Charles T. Lanham, Reid's chief of staff; Black newspaper publisher John H. Sengstacke; William H. Stevenson, president of Oberlin College; Kenneth Royall, Secretary of the Army; Stuart Symington, Secretary of the Air Force; Lester Granger, executive secretary of the Urban League; business executive Dwight R. G. Palmer; John L. Sullivan, Secretary of the Navy; and Charles Fahy, chairman of the President's Committee on Equality of Treatment and Opportunity in the Armed Services, also known as the Fahy Committee. *Truman Library*

4. All executive departments and agencies of the Federal Government are authorized and directed to cooperate with the Committee in its work, and to furnish the Committee such information or the services of such persons as the Committee may require in the performance of its duties.

5. When requested by the Committee to do so, persons in the armed services or in any of the executive departments and agencies of the Federal Government shall testify before the Committee and shall make available for use of the Committee such documents and other information as the Committee may require.

6. The Committee shall continue to exist until such time as the President shall terminate its existence by Executive order.

> [signed]
> Harry Truman
> The White House
> July 26, 1948

Secretary of the Army Kenneth Royall and a group of black newspaper publishers, together in Europe of a tour of an army installation, 19 March, 1948. Left to right: Thomas W. Young, editor, *Norfolk Journal and Guide*; Carter Wesley, publisher, *Houston Informer*; Frank J. Stanley, publisher, *Louisville Defender*; William G. Nunn, managing editor, *Pittsburgh Courier*; Louis Martin, editor, *Chicago Defender*; Cliff W. MacKay, assistant editor, *Afro-American Newspapers*; and Dowdal H. Davis, managing editor, *Kansas City Call*. *National Archives*

Segregation officially ended in the active armed forces with the announcement of the Secretary of Defense in 1954 that the last all-black unit had been disbanded. In the little more than six years after President Truman's order, some quarter of a million blacks had been intermingled with whites in the nation's military units worldwide. These changes ushered in a brief era of good feeling during which the services and the civil rights advocates tended to overlook some forms of discrimination that persisted within the services. This tendency became even stronger in the early 1960s when the discrimination suffered by black servicemen in local communities dramatized the relative effectiveness of the equal treatment and opportunity policies on military installations. In July 1963, in the wake of another presidential investigation of racial equality in the armed forces, Secretary of Defense [Robert] McNamara outlined a new racial policy. An extension of the forces that had produced the abolition of segregated units, the new policy also vowed to carry the crusade for equal treatment and opportunity for black servicemen outside the military compound into the civilian community beyond. McNamara's 1963 directive became the model for subsequent racial orders in the Defense Department.

Source: MacGregor, Morris J., Jr. Integration of the Armed Forces: 1940–1965. Washington, D.C.: United States Department of Defense, Center of Military History, 1981.

Surrounded by black leaders looking on, President Truman signs a proclamation commemorating the abolition of slavery, 1 July, 1948. Later that month he would issue his own history-making Executive Order 9981. *National Archives*

Social events remained informally segregated long after Executive Order 9981 was issued, evidenced here by this army base dance for blacks at Fort George Meade, Maryland, June 1952. *National Archives*

Integration in action, on display in this line of inductees, Fort Sam Houston, Texas, 1953. *U.S. Army*

This gesture—the offering of a cigarette and a light near Khe Sanh, 1968—says something of the advances made since Truman's executive order to integrate the armed forces. *U.S. Marine Corps*

The Black Experience in Korea

Soldiers man a front-line outpost near Kaejun, Korea, 22 November 1950. *U.S. Army*

The intelligence and reconnaissance platoon of the 24th Infantry, Korea, May 1951. *U.S. Army*

Men of the 9th Infantry Regiment evacuate wounded soldiers from Hill 201, Korea. *U.S. Army*

A desegregated steward's training class at Great Lakes Naval Training Center, Illinois, 13 April 1953. *National Archives*

Black and white troops work together to assist a medical evacuation, Korea, 5 September 1951. *National Archives*

Black and white troops of the 2nd Infantry, Korea, 20 November 1950. *National Archives*

The Vietnam War, 1965–1972

America's first racially integrated war effort took place in the Southeast Asian country of Vietnam between 1965 and 1972. Of the 58,148 American troops who died in Vietnam and the 304,000 wounded, 22 percent were black against a stateside population of only 11 percent. Less than 3 percent of army and 1 percent of marine commissioned officers serving in Vietnam were black, although the conflict produced twenty black Medal of Honor winners and brilliant leaders like Gen. Colin Powell, who would later become chairman of the Joint Chiefs and U.S. Secretary of State. Thus, the confusing and often contradictory legacy of Vietnam and Black Power was born.

U.S. Air Force nurse Lt. Linda Bowser attends to a young girl in the village of Bong Son on 10 January 1974. The American presence ended with the evacuation of Saigon in April 1975.
National Archives

A black soldier holds a Vietnamese orphan.
National Archives

At no time in American history did black soldiers, sailors, and marines have more voices—from those of nonviolent civil-rights leader Dr. Martin Luther King Jr. and black Muslim separatist minister Malcolm X to those of Student Nonviolent Coordinating Committee (SNCC) leader Stokely Charmichael and Black Panther Eldridge Cleaver—sounding in their ears during the late 1960s. With the influx of often illiterate black recruits (41 percent of 246,000 total black recruits) arriving under President Lyndon Johnson's "Project 100,000," joining black enlistees and draftees already in country between 1966 and 1969, the battle was on for the heart and soul of the black troops serving in Vietnam.

While racist white troops flew Confederate flags from their vehicles and quarters, black troops responded with Black Panther accessories, including beads, t-shirts, and berets, and flew black flags as race relations deteriorated rapidly in

We must concentrate not merely on the negative expulsion of war but the positive affirmation of peace.

—Rev. Dr. Martin Luther King, Jr., 1967

A black Marine with I Company displays determination in a search for the enemy eight miles north of Da Nang, Vietnam, on 30 October 1969. *National Archives*

The United States government is the greatest purveyor of violence in the world today.

—Rev. Dr. Martin Luther King Jr., 1967

A black soldier awaits an ambush in the Vietnam jungle. *National Archives*

Vietnam between 1966 and 1969. Race riots raged on military posts, at base camps, and even on aircraft carriers, such as on the USS *Kitty Hawk* in the Tonkin Gulf, when a disturbance left thirty-three sailors injured. Morale deteriorated along with race relations, and drug use and desertions skyrocketed among both black and white troops. The South Alley section of Saigon was home to 300 to 500 black troops away without leave (AWOL) between 1967 and 1969 until the army changed policies of racial discrimination that began reversing the AWOL trend in 1969.

Vietnam: Spooky Death From Above

For E-6 Sgt. Richard Paul Harrell, Vietnam service meant death from above for thousands of enemy troops courtesy of his AC-47 "Spooky" gunship. Born in Gadsden, Alabama, in 1945, Harrell attended Morehouse College before enlisting in the U.S. Air Force at Lackland Air Force Base, Texas, in 1963 and receiving aviation mechanics training at Sheppard Air Force Base, Texas. In 1964, Harrell arrived at Ismir Air Force Base, Turkey, where he received flight-engineer training and qualified, although he lacked the formal training.

Harrell trained in a T-39 passenger plane and a Convair 131 medevac aircraft under NATO control and participated in a number of dangerous covert missions, carrying military brass and diplomats across Europe, with weekly stops in Athens,

Greece. After a short stateside stint at Richard Gabaur Air Force Base in Missouri, where he received training on a C-118 cargo plane, he was shipped to Vietnam in the fall of 1967.

"We arrived during monsoon season and, upon seeing Binh Thuot Air Force Base, I remember wondering why anyone would build an airfield in the middle of a lake," Harrell recalled. "There were so many blacks on the ground crews there and at neighboring Can Tho Army base that I thought I was back in Alabama.

"While in camp and several days after the funeral of Rev. Martin Luther King Jr., we [blacks] were playing poker and a group of white Southern soldiers approached. They asked 'if we wanted to buy some mules from that nigger's funeral.' The resulting fight was bloody, and we got the best of it as we were not going to take no mess from nobody!" (Harrell 2008).

Harrell's new assignment was one of the most lethal airplanes in the USAF arsenal. The AC-47 "Spooky" gunship could fire up to 6,000 7.62 rounds per minute, and a three-second burst could cover a football field with bullets every two inches. The AC-47 fire was directed by troops on the ground, aimed from the cockpit, and delivered from a left bank.

Harrell's AC-47 flew combat air patrol (CAP) missions nightly in and around the Delta region, with a second gunship on standby for a fifteen-minute turnaround. The planes provided cover fire for infantry operations, Agent Orange drops, and downed helicopters and airplanes and were rarely hit by ground fire from enemy, who could not figure out the lead for a left-banking aircraft.

Flying only at night, Harrell made his first combat mission to the Seven Mountains region near the Cambodian border, where U.S. Marines were under attack while defending a village and a large force of enemy troops was attempting to overrun them. Flying between 500 and 1,000 feet and firing 3 million candle-bright flares to illuminate the enemy, Harrell's AC-47 killed hundreds of the enemy in mere seconds and saved the Marine force on the ground.

He would later earn a Distinguished Flying Cross with two oak-leaf clusters for a mission south of Nha Trang, where U.S. Special Forces were under fire from a large enemy force.

"We caught them [NVA troops] in a rice paddy and had 350 confirmed kills that night, as our fire was very accurate and the death toll was actually much higher with drag offs. We had good weather, so the pilot could hold us steady to hit our target," said Harrell.

"Although we saved our soldiers, I have always grieved for the loved ones of the 350 men we killed that night, who would never come home again."

As I look back at the things we did in Vietnam, I think of the children that were murdered and brutalized by the Viet Cong and sometimes our own troops. . . . I hate war because it is so inhumane.

—Sgt. Richard P. Harrell

Korean War

Since President Harry Truman's 1948 Executive Order integrating the military was largely ignored by commanders, the 24th Infantry remained segregated throughout the Korean War and included the only two black Medal of Honor recipients. **Sgt. Cornelius Charlton** led his men to repulse an enemy attack with grenades and machine gun fire until he was killed near Chipo-ri, 1951, while **Pfc. William Henry Thompson** sacrificed himself to allow his unit to escape near Haman, 1950.

William Henry Thompson   James Anderson Jr.

Vietnam War

Twenty black troops received the Medal of Honor during the Vietnam War, including U.S. Marine **Pfc. James Anderson Jr.**, 3rd Marine Division, who smothered a grenade to save other Marines, Cam Lo, 1967. **Staff Sgt. Webster Anderson** of the 320th Artillery Regiment, 101st Airborne led defense of his position although severely wounded, Tam Ky, 1967.

Sgt. **Eugene Ashley Jr.** of the 5th Special Forces Group led five assaults against the enemy before being killed in the Battle of Lang Vei, 1968, while Marine **Pfc. Oscar Austin**, 7th Marines, gave his life to save a wounded trooper, Da Nang, 1969. **Sgt. William Maud Bryant**, 5th Special Forces, was killed by an enemy rocket after leading repeated attacks on enemy bunkers at Long Khanh Province, 1969, while Marine **Sgt. Rodney Davis** (1st Marines, Quang Nam Province, 1967) and **Pfc. Robert Jenkins Jr.** (3rd Marines, Fire Support Base Argonne, DMZ, 1969) smothered grenades to save their men.

Sgt. **Lawrence Joel** of the 503rd Infantry treated injured soldiers while wounded in 1965, while **Sgt. Dwight Johnson**, 69th Armored Regiment, repeatedly attacked the enemy at Dak To, 1968. Marine **Pfc. Ralph Johnson** (1st Marines, Hill

Rodney Davis   Lawrence Joel

146, Quan Duc Valley, 1968), **Pfc. Garfield Langhorn** (17th Cavalry, Phi Djereng, Pleiku Province, 1969), **Pfc. Donald Russell Long** (4th Cavalry, 1966), and **Pfc. Milton Olive III** (503rd Infantry, Phu Cuong, 1965) all smothered grenades to save their men.

Sgt. **Matthew Leonard**, 16th Infantry, Suoi Da, 1967, fought while severely wounded; **Capt. Riley Pitts**, 25th

| Dwight Johnson | Donald Russell Long | Milton Olive III | Matthew Leonard |

| Riley Pitts | Charles Calvin Rogers | Clarence Sasser | John Warren, Jr. |

Infantry Division, Ap Dong, 1967, led his men valiantly against the enemy; and **Lt. Col. Charles Calvin Rogers**, 5th Artillery Regiment, 1st Division, Cambodian border, 1968, held command even while severely wounded, defeating the enemy.

Lt. Ruppert Sargent, 25th Infantry Division, Hau Nghia Province, 1967, and **Staff Sgt. Clifford Chester Simms**, 101st Airborne, Hue, 1968, both smothered grenades to save their men as **Pfc. Clarence Sasser**, 60th Infantry, Ding Tuong Province, 1968, administered first aid to wounded troops, ignoring his own injuries for five hours until evacuated. **Lt. John Warren Jr.**, 25th Infantry Division, Tay Ninh Province, 1969, treated wounded until he was killed by the enemy.

Vietnam: Ambush at A Shau Valley

Eighteen-year-old U.S. Marine Pfc. Clarence Burnough completed sixteen weeks of basic training at Paris Island, South Carolina, before arriving in Vietnam in October 1968 with 3rd Division, Echo Company. He received an immediate introduction to enemy fire.

> We were dropped off to company and twenty minutes later were under mortar and small-arms fire, and we didn't know what to do. After the attack, [a lieutenant] told us to "fall back and follow whatever somebody's doing in front of you until you're told differently."
>
> Later, on my first patrol on the same day, I was hacking my way through jungle when [I was] confronted with a North Vietnamese soldier. As he started shooting at me, I thought of my training and the "let them shoot first" Geneva Convention. I was so scared I fell backwards, firing all the rounds from my M-16 weapon and, amazingly, hit him ten times in sheer terror.
>
> I remember later writing my mother and telling her how I had to kill this guy today. The incident changed me that day, and after that it was a dog-eat-dog, survival-of-the-fittest mentality for me. Once you do that [kill] you don't have feeling anymore other than cold, so it doesn't matter if you're face-to-face or a

Private First Class Clarence Burnough at home after sixteen weeks of basic training at Paris Island, prior to embarkation to Vietnam with the 3rd Marine Division, Echo Company, in the fall of 1968.

Whenever God is ready for us, he is going to take us. . . . [I]t took me a long time to get to that point in Vietnam. He was there, but I still wonder why it had to happen?

—Pfc. Clarence Burnough, 1992

Left to right, author Robert V. Morris with Clarence Burnough and William Morris during production of the documentary for PBS/Iowa Public Television, *Tradition and Valor*, Des Moines, Iowa, 1993.

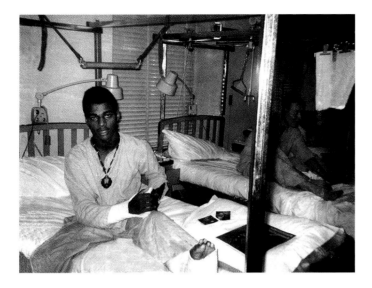

Burnough as a patient at Great Lakes Naval Hospital, Illinois, in 1969, where he was interviewed by CBS newsman Walter Cronkite, but had little to say.

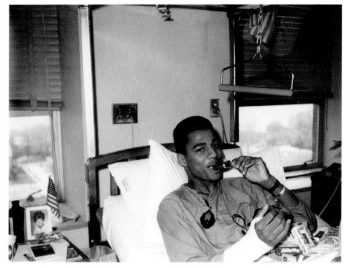

Burnough got to eat plenty of ice cream doing his recovery at Great Lakes Naval Hospital, in Illinois, in 1969. Through thirty-three surgeries and fifteen blood transfusions, he gradually gained strength in his shattered (but reattached) leg and arm, and made a full recovery.

mile away. I was out there to kill somebody or be killed, and that's what I did best at the time.

I was surprised by the racial tension during that time, as I met a lot of black Marines and army guys who felt that Vietnam racial relations were just an extension of [those in] the United States. Not a whole lot changed the black-white situation. White marines still called black marines "boy" and other demeaning things that often were settled in combat. There were a lot of things that went on over there that the American public is not aware of. The government has its own way of handling things, and if it's not on paper, then it didn't happen.

My first squad of fourteen men included ten blacks, and we were together all the time. The few white guys fit right in, as we were trying to help each other survive. Between the enemy, the heat and other climate conditions, and survival itself, there were a lot more important issues to deal with than race.

My favorite duty was working as a sniper, as I was one of five men selected from Echo Company about a month after my arrival. Every night we would go out with infrared [starlight] scopes for what we called "hanging out." We would get up in a tree or on a mountain and just kind of wait on them [the NVA] as we knew they would be doing reconnaissance. Sometimes we would be after specific people, like officers or enemy snipers.

Soldiers apply first aid to a fellow serviceman who was wounded in a mine explosion, Vietnam, April 1968. *U.S. Army*

It calls for a different emotion to put the X on somebody's head, as it is a one-on-one kill, but I was out there to kill someone or be killed, and that's what I did. (Burnough 1992)

Echo Company experienced heavy combat against the enemy in the Oklahoma Hills of Quang Tri Province, where they chased "rock apes" away—the dangerous A Shau Valley. Operation Dewey Canyon, from 22 January to 18 March 1969, would cost 130 Marines killed and 932 wounded, including Burnough on 15 March. Confirmed enemy deaths were only 1,600.

Our Operation Dewey Canyon objective was to reach hill 937, and the L-shaped NVA ambush was set, and we got blown to pieces, with a lot of people going up in their color groceries. . . . nothing coming down but legs, arms, and heads. I got shot in both legs, my left side, and right arm. The radio man in front of me got hit about eighteen times, and his body just went mangled. Fortunately, I was still conscious and within reach of his radio to call for help.

Fearing helicopter attack, the NVA pulled out, except for two men they left to check and rob us. Those were the last two people I killed in Vietnam as, when they flipped me over, I shot them both with my .45-caliber pistol.

As I had laid there with the NVA coming, I prepared myself for their arrival. I had a flashback of my whole life, from kindergarten up to where I was then. I thought about everyone that I thought cared about me and who I cared about, the foods I liked to eat, and other thoughts.

When the Marine medics got to us, I was in a lot of pain. My left leg was almost off, and the bone in my right arm was blown out and laying on the ground near me. It took the medivac helicopters a little time to get there, but they finally did and got the survivors out.

Through it all I never thought I was going to die, although I should have. After two blood transfusions and numerous operations, they wanted to take my left leg off, and I refused. I told them that I wanted to keep it even if I had to drag it, so they had to grow the bone back at a slant. They took part of my hip for [a] bone graft and ran a rod through my arm, but I regained my ability to walk. (Burnough 1992)

After fragment removal at Quang Tri Province, Burnough's medical journey included major surgeries at Japan, Guam, and eventually the Great Lakes Naval Hospital and Walter Reed Army Medical Center.

CBS newsman Walter Cronkite interviewed Burnough on his feelings about the war when Burnough was at Great Lakes Naval Hospital in 1969. But the private was surprised and had few comments.

"I told him [Cronkite] that I was just trying to get my life together, and I didn't have comments on a lot of things he asked me because I really hadn't thought about it. All I wanted was to get back home, eat some soul food, and go to college," Burnough recalled.

But forty years later, Burnough did have an opinion about the war—and a strong one. When interviewed in 1992 for Iowa Public Television, he said, "Vietnam was a political war and a tremendous waste of lives on both sides." (Burnough 1992)

Staff Sergeant Melvin G. Gaines after a brutal several-hour search of Viet Cong tunnels, 17 March 1967. *U.S. Army*

Platoon Sergeant John Martindale issues hurried instructions to his men as their unit prepares to set up a defensive perimeter, South Vietnam, August 1971. *U.S. Army*

Members of Company C, 5th Battalion, 9th Infantry cross a channel during Operation Hot Tac, northeast of My Tho, Vietnam, 6 April 1967. *U.S. Army*

The Black Experience in Vietnam

A machine gunner, 3rd Battalion, 187th Airborne Infantry Regiment, 101st Airborne Division, defends a position in the A Shau Valley, 30 September 1969. *U.S. Army*

The men of the 173rd Airborne Brigade embark on a "search-and-destroy" mission, Phouc Tuy, June 1966. *U.S. Army*

Brigadier General Frederick E. Davison, commanding general of the 199th Light Infantry Brigade (left), congratulates Maj. Gen. Fillmore K. Mearne, commander, Capital Military Assistance Command, for his Distinguished Service Medal, April 1969. *U.S. Army*

American Marines at the Forward Command Post in Hue City, 23 February 1968. *Terry Fincher/Express/Getty Images*

Men of the 35th Infantry on patrol during Operation Baker, Vietnam, May 1967. *U.S. Army*

Frank E. Petersen of the United States Marine Corps boards a McDonnell Douglas F-4 Phantom II, circa 1968. In 1979, he became the first African-American Marine Corps general. *Pictorial Parade/Archive Photos/Getty Images*

CHAPTER 8

The Modern Era and the Evolution of Black Leadership

William M. Johnson (center), division command sergeant major of 1st Armored Division, out of Wiesbaden, Germany, along with James P. Daniels (right), command sergeant major of 1st Brigade Combat Team, 1st Armored Division ("Ready First"), out of Fort Bliss, Texas, in Kirkuk, Iraq, May 15, 2010. *U.S. Army*

Brigadier General Arnold N. Gordon-Bray is former deputy commanding general at the United States Army Cadet Command in Fort Monroe, Virginia. Gordon-Bray is a native of South Carolina. He graduated from Waynesville High School, Waynesville, Missouri, in 1973. He was commissioned in the infantry, as a distinguished military student, through the ROTC program at Central Missouri State University in 1978. He holds a bachelor of science degree from Central Missouri State University and master's degrees in international strategic studies from the United States Air War College in Montgomery, Alabama, and the Naval War College in Newport, Rhode Island. He completed the infantry officer basic and advanced courses, jungle operations course, U.S. Army Command and General Staff College, Combined Arms Services and Staff College, Armed Forces Staff College—JPME II, NATO Staff Officer's Course, Air War College, Naval War College, and numerous other military schools.

Gordon-Bray's command assignments include brigade commander, 2nd Brigade of the 82nd Airborne Division (Falcon Brigade), where he changed command in Baghdad on 6 July 2003 after more than twenty-five months; battalion commander of the 1st Battalion, 508th Airborne Combat Team, in Vicenza, Italy, from 1996 to 1998; commander of A Company, 1st Battalion, 501st Parachute Infantry Regiment; and commander, Headquarters and Headquarters Company, 502nd Infantry Regiment, 101st Airborne Division (Air Assault), in Fort Campbell, Kentucky.

Gordon-Bray's other positions include chief of the Preliminary Marksmanship Committee, in Fort Jackson, South Carolina; infantry platoon leader assignments in Alpha and Combat Support Companies of the 1st Battalion, 9th Infantry, 2nd Infantry Division, at Camp Liberty Bell, Korea; battalion operations officer of the 2nd Battalion, 502nd Infantry Regiment, in the 101st Airborne Division (Air Assault), at Fort Campbell, Kentucky; aide-de-camp to the commander, XVIII Airborne Corps; and battalion operations officer and executive officer with the 2nd Battalion, 504th Parachute Infantry Regiment, and chief of training in the Joint Special Operations Command—all three at Fort Bragg, North Carolina; deputy chief of the Planning Group for the commander of Training and Doctrine Command (TRADOC), in Fort Monroe, Virginia; and professor of Joint Military Operations at the Naval War College.

Prior to his current assignment, Gordon-Bray completed his second tour in Iraq as the principal advisor to the Iraqi Ground Force commander in 2007. He returned to Fort Monroe, where he served as the director of the Joint and Army Experimentation Division and was one of the founding members of the Futures Center and Army Capabilities Integration Center (ARCIC), Training and Doctrine Command (from 2003 to 2006).

Gordon-Bray has been awarded the Expert Infantryman's Badge, Combat Infantryman's Badge, Combat Action Badge, Master Parachutist Badge, Air Assault Badge, the Ranger tab, and various foreign parachutist badges, including German Master Wings. Among his medals are the Legion of Merit (with oak-leaf cluster), the Bronze Star (second award), Defense Meritorious Service, Meritorious Service Medal (seventh award), Humanitarian Service, Joint Meritorious Unit Award, and the Saint Maurice (primicerius) and Saint Barbara's Medals for Infantry and Artillery Excellence.

Here, Gordon-Bray writes about the ongoing evolution of leadership and the inclusion of African-American personnel in the military.

In recent years, there has been a tremendous increase in the responsibility of command for people of color in the military. The cultural evolution in the military is hard to capture in mere words and pictures, although the hard work and struggles are often evident in the faces. Those depicted in this chapter have, and are, truly standing on the shoulders and achievements of previous generations; the Vietnam era set the stage for a seismic shift.

By the end of the Vietnam War, African Americans had demonstrated potential to both fight and lead. All minorities, but African-Americans in particular, achieved significant acceptance and gains during the post-Vietnam era. To help set the stage for the black faces in this chapter, it is important to understand the environment, the impacts on the population, and some of the policies that enabled change.

The Strategic Environment

Following the Vietnam Conflict, the U.S. Army went into a period of redefinition reflective of the national strategic interests and political tolerance of the 1970s. While curtailing the spread of communism and preserving democracy was still paramount in the minds of the national leadership, reasonable minds had concluded that the greater threat to the United States was defeating the Russians (the Union of Soviet Socialist Republics, or USSR) in Europe and stopping the spread of the Russian agenda around the world, and in doing so, trying to overtly fight communist forces in Southeast Asia.

To address the European contingencies against the USSR, three U.S. corps were positioned in Europe, ready to support the North Atlantic Treaty Organization (NATO) allies for this envisioned tough and potentially catastrophic fight. A third corps was maintained in the United States to augment the USSR threat. Generally,

Brigadier General Arnold N. Gordon-Bray.
U.S. Army

Brigadier General Arnold N. Gordon-Bray poses with a Buffalo Soldiers flag in Iraq.
Courtesy Brigadier General Arnold N. Gordon-Bray

the best senior commanders and most prepared lieutenants were assigned to the European threat or to elite units—a process that really continued until the 1990s.

The secondary fight for the U.S. Army was focused on the Korean peninsula. The armistice of 1953 left U.S. forces still committed in support of our Korean allies along the demilitarized zone (DMZ) between North and South Korea. To address the secondary threat, a corps-sized force in Korea and another stationed in the United States were tasked against this threat and possible spin-offs for other Pacific Rim contingencies. The third area of concern has become the most prevalent today—peace operations and counterinsurgency conflicts. The embers of opposing ideologies around the world, which may or may not have real or recognized state sponsorship, have been around a long time, but following the dissolution of the USSR in 1990, a once-bifurcated world opened up opportunities for myriad military operations and conflicts.

Brigadier General Arnold N. Gordon-Bray sticks his head out of the notorious "spider hole" in which Saddam Hussein was found. *Courtesy Brigadier General Arnold N. Gordon-Bray*

These later conflicts, which I will simply call army operations, have been called operations other than war, covert operations, special operations, guerilla operations, constabulatory operations, or components of the peace operations. Whatever the name, these operations were usually initially addressed by the army's contingency corps, special forces, airborne forces, U.S. Marines, U.S. State Department elements, and/or some interagency elements. Because of the immediate nature, low visibility, and usually small amount of forces required, the army placed emphasis on light, highly deployable units and very athletic soldiers within the units.

Inclusion and Leadership

The Vietnam Conflict did more than change the military strategy; it changed the United States military and its relationship with the civilian population in ways that no other conflict had. America no longer had all parts of America in its ranks by the end of the Vietnam War. The lack of popularity of the Vietnam War and the selective-service draft employed left the army as a place for already career soldiers, Americans who had a military propensity, former military dependents, or those who were socio-economically challenged.

The chasm between America and the collective of America was at an all-time low. The national wounds of Vietnam forced the army into establishing a 500,000-plus, all-volunteer force (a volunteer army, or VOLAR) to support its global security requirements. To get the soldiers and leadership needed, all of the desirous American population had to be available for employment. Racism, although lessened in the 1970s and 1980s, continued in America, but tales of equality within the army, and evidenced by enlisted promotions, demonstrated that the army was a place for increased opportunity for African Americans.

Black soldiers who were stationed overseas were viewed as Americans first and, therefore, experienced less overt prejudice than they did in most parts of the United States. Consequently many of the very talented junior African-American leaders believed that their full worth was better realized in the army, and they remained in the army in numbers disproportionate to those of their white counterparts. Moreover, Vietnam provided a heavy infusion of reserve officers, in addition to enlisted soldiers with high school diplomas.

The real impacts of Vietnam came to fruition in the number African Americans commanding companies, battalions, brigades, and even larger formations and most significantly in the number of general officers in the late 1970s, 1980s, and 1990s. By the late 1990s and into the millennium, there were unprecedented numbers of black division and corps commanders serving with some regularity relative to the numbers available during and immediately following Vietnam. Ironically, by the mid-1980s, as the economy provided more opportunities for African Americans in the civilian sector, black officers were pursuing the combat arms. The impact of fewer black officers, and specifically combat-arms leaders, has resulted in an essentially stagnant percentage of general officers (around 10 percent overall and 6 percent with the combat arms) since 1979.

U.S. Army Sergeant Charles Snow of Columbia, South Carolina, on guard outside Bagram District Courthouse, Ghulam Ali, Parwan Province, Afghanistan, on May 18, 2010. *U.S. Army*

A U.S. Army NCO gives the latest update to service members just after an attack on Bagram Airfield, Afghanistan. Insurgents attacked Bagram Airfield with small arms fire, grenades, and rocket-propelled grenades on May 19, 2010. *U.S. Army*

U.S. soldiers attached to the 17th Fires Brigade speak to local citizens in Az Zubayr, Iraq, on May 12, 2010, while an Iraqi soldier provides added security. The soldiers discussed security and economic issues with the Iraqis. *U.S. Army*

Service and Policy

The mid and late 1970s was still a period of open racial struggle in America. Military operations around the world forced soldiers to integrate holistically, and although the army was not immune to racial challenges, it outpaced virtually every major industry in America with diversity examples at the senior levels. The influx of black officers from the Vietnam era suggests that getting more black general officers would happen naturally; however, most leaders agree it really wasn't until the appointment of African Americans into the civilian military leadership, with people like Clifford Alexander (1977) and his insistence on policy changes for equal opportunity, that full inclusion began to occur.

Officer and enlisted levels of representation are still markedly different because African Americans have not joined the combat-arms branches and civilian opportunities for entrepreneurs and industry have increased. To date, there has never been an African-American army (or any other service) chief of staff, and Gene C. McKinney, who served as tenth sergeant major of the army (SMA) from 1995 through 1997, was the first and is still the only African-American to serve as SMA.

Chris Johnson of Springfield, Virginia, performs pull-ups for Staff Sgt. Marlon Green, a drill sergeant from Houston, Texas, during the Joint Service Open House and Air Show at Andrews Air Base, Maryland, on May 15, 2010. Green entertained people waiting in line to play the America's Army Virtual Army Experience combat simulator by making sure they were in the best shape for duty. *U.S. Army*

A Transitioning Army

As European nations begin to assert their own economic independence in the late 1990s, leading U.S. forces to have an increasingly smaller presence outside of the United States, the U.S. Army began to establish a continental-U.S.-based army. In the new millennium, the army was converting to a more tailorable, modular force that was more deployable and had blended capability between light and mechanized forces. African Americans were involved in the design of the new army on the drawing board and the battlefield: in 1995, Maj. Gen. Montague Winfield performed the first operational field test of the digitally linked mechanized forces, and Col. Julius Coates was the director of the design-and-training team responsible for the concept.

Leadership and Inclusion of Women in the Army: 1974–1994

Brigadier General Clara L. Adams-Ender, U.S. Army (ret.), enlisted as a private in the Women's Army Corps Reserve in 1959, when she received a scholarship to complete her last two years of undergraduate nursing education. This is her account of her service and of the evolving role of women in the military.

The army was experiencing a shortage of nurses, so they sponsored an army student-nurse program to assist nursing students in completing their education in exchange for two to three years on active duty upon graduation. The program paid tuition, room, and board and a monthly stipend of $250. Three months before graduation, I was commissioned as a second lieutenant in the U.S. Army Nurse Corps.

Upon entry onto active duty, I attended the officer basic course, then served in a series of assignments as an intensive-care/recovery-room nurse to gain nursing skills and to increase my experience as a specialty nurse. In my first seven years of active duty, I had a tour overseas, attended a course in intensive-care nursing, attended the nursing advanced course, and obtained a master's degree. In the next three years, I had taught army medics and was teaching nursing in the army's school of nursing.

Since I was commissioned as an army Nurse Corps officer in the army's Medical Department, I was a part of the special-branch army and not the line army. Upon learning this fact, I immediately learned about who were considered to be leaders and who were not. First, the army Nurse Corps branch was about 95 percent female at that time, and women's work was not valued and respected and was often not even recognized. Moreover, since females in

Portrait of Brig. Gen. Clara Adams-Ender, circa 1993. *U.S. Army*

the army comprised only about 3 percent of the total force, I learned quickly that women were largely ignored.

In 1974, I was assigned to a leadership position in the Nurse Corps. The position was assistant chief, Department of Nursing, at Fort Meade, Maryland. By this time in my career, I was very well grounded in my profession, and I had made some decisions and formed some opinions about my value and worth in the health-care world that were much more positive than what I perceived the army thought of me.

I learned early in the army that command positions were looked upon as the only leadership positions. Any position less than command was considered to be a staff position and somehow lesser than being commander. In the 1970s, army nurses were not allowed to assume command positions, so the avenues to leadership, as perceived by the army, were not opened to nurses. A glimmer of hope appeared, however, in 1970, when the first females were promoted to the rank of brigadier general. The level of brigadier general quickly became the glass ceiling that was not to be broken for several more years. Four stars for women would have been laughable.

Since army nurses were specifically prohibited from holding command positions, we went about our performance of duties in our staff positions to the best of our ability. Our ultimate mission was to provide quality nursing care to soldiers in times of war and peace in support of the overall army mission. Although I believed that army nurses had an important and vital mission, I also believed that the army leadership made a concerted and deliberate effort to exclude women from assuming any leadership positions. Further, my perception was that this discriminatory practice was based largely upon gender—a factor over which the women had no control.

In 1975, I was promoted to the rank of lieutenant colonel before my year group and was considered to be on a fast track. I was selected to be the one nurse officer to attend the Command and General Staff College that year and graduated in the class of 1976—the bicentennial year. That same year was identified by the Department of Defense as the International Year for Women. The department directed that each command specifically recognize the contributions of women and set goals for the overall advancement of women in the ranks. From my "foxhole," I saw little progress being made in the movement of women into command positions. There were a few nurses who achieved senior-level positions on staffs in some line commands; these were few and far between. The prohibition for nurses in command still held. For the most part, it seemed that women were an invisible minority that was tolerated when needed, but largely ignored as a group.

The Women's Army Corps (WAC) was disbanded as a separate branch of the army in 1978. Many women lost command opportunities that they were afforded in the corps. However, the increase in the numbers of women in the ranks of the line army meant that they worked side-by-side with men, doing their jobs. The dynamics were interesting and often revealing. It was soon learned that these women came to get jobs done and, in many instances, out-performed the men. As a result, they began to question why they had to be led by men who performed less well as they in some instances. The Defense Advisory Committee on Women in the Services (DACOWITS) studied this issue for a long time and made recommendations that resulted in women being allowed to command in all line units except infantry, armor, and some field-artillery units. This was a significant turning point in army-leadership history.

My own career was still flourishing, although the army nurse restriction from command remained in the mid-1980s. I was selected below the zone to full colonel and became chief nurse of the largest medical center in the Department of Defense in 1984. At this time, I had many opportunities to interface with Department of Army staff in the Pentagon. I taught them much about my job responsibilities at a large medical center, and I learned from them what it meant to be assigned at the Pentagon. In 1984, I was selected for promotion to brigadier general and to be chief of the Army Nurse Corps. In my new position, I assumed administrative and managerial responsibilities for 22,000 nurses serving all over the world. (This number of personnel is larger than that of an army division.) In addition, the surgeon general appointed me to be director of personnel as an additional duty. In this position, I had administrative and managerial responsibilities for the 100,000 health-care professionals, serving all over the world, in the army Medical Department. This was the first time in history that a nurse had held such a position. I pursued the position for two reasons: the surgeon general needed a general officer to take responsibility for personnel issues, and I needed the additional 200 personnel in the personnel directorate to help me manage army Nurse Corps officers. It all worked out beautifully.

When I became chief of the army Nurse Corps, I was immediately assigned to the Department of Army staff. That was a helpful move, because I moved in more circles with line-army officers, especially generals. I could continue to educate them and other influential civilian personnel about the leadership expertise of army Nurse Corps officers. I learned all too quickly that other army Medical Department officers who had served alongside line officers for many years had given the line officers erroneous perceptions of the roles and responsibilities of nurses in health care. I embarked on an intensive education and training program and also solicited the aid and assistance of some of my former bosses from my recruiting days. By this time, two of them were vice chief of staff and deputy chief of staff for personnel. They provided credibility and legitimacy to my story, and soon the respect for nurses began flourishing.

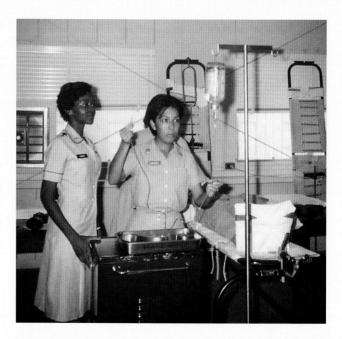

Clara Adams-Ender (left) instructs a student in IV use during a medical-surgical nursing course at U.S. Army Medical Training Center, Fort Sam Houston, Texas, circa 1964. *U.S. Army*

Change came for me and the army in 1991, when I was leaving my position as chief of the army Nurse Corps. At that time, according to Title 10, U.S. Code, the army Nurse Corps chief could serve for only four years and attain the rank of brigadier general. If she or he desired to remain on active duty, he or she would have had to revert to the rank of colonel to serve longer. As I was preparing for my retirement, I received a call from the general officer of the Management Office, who said that if I were willing, the army chief of staff would petition Congress for me to remain on active duty and move on to another assignment. The action of transferring an officer from the special-branch army to the line army would be historical—it had been done only once before in army history.

I later had a conversation with the chief, and he told me that I had had an outstanding career, but had not done enough for the army to that point. I reminded him that I had managed and administered to a group of nurses larger than a division. He said to me, "Clara, that was administration and management. To validate your real value to the army, you must serve in a command position. I'm going to send you down to command Fort Belvoir [in Virginia]. Don't screw it up!" I knew exactly what that statement meant, and it added to the pressure that I felt as I anticipated the assignment. I was keenly aware of the fact that I was a woman and, specifically, an African-American woman. By this time in my career, I had faced the reality that my gender and race seemed to be obstacles preventing some leaders from offering me new opportunities. If I went down to Fort Belvoir, did something illegal, and got relieved, it would be a long time before another woman, especially an African-American woman, would be placed in a command position again. I felt like I would be carrying the full weight of the future of army women generals in command on my shoulders. I would have been more stressed and fearful had I not been a nurse. A nurse's responsibility is to diagnose and treat a patient's responses to real or imagined health problems. They must learn and practice skills that prepare them for such stresses. They are taught a process of managing difficult situations using the steps of assessment, planning, intervention, and evaluation to arrive at satisfactory conclusions. Instead of feeling panic, I just started the process in my head, and soon I had a basic plan of how to cope with the pending situation.

In addition to commanding Fort Belvoir, I was also the deputy commander of the Military District of Washington. In that role, I assisted the commander with the myriad of duties required to be the executive agent for all military ceremonies for the president and all other dignitaries in the Washington metropolitan area.

Throughout my military career, I had been educated and trained to command and lead troops. I am grateful to the chief of staff for giving me the opportunity to prove that I could do it according to army standards. As a result of my successful tenure as Fort Belvoir commander, the prohibition to command for nurses was lifted, and they now command military hospitals and other health-care units.

My experiences in command did provide me with more diverse experiences and the opportunity to influence the lives of many people, which I would never have experienced as a nurse manager. I am also proud of the fact that the army leadership awarded me the Distinguished Service Medal with oak-leaf cluster (second award) for my performance of duty.

Clara Adams-Ender stands outside the tent that served as Post Operative Ward 2 at a field hospital in South Korea in 1964. *U.S. Army*

Afghanistan (Operation Enduring Freedom, 2001–) and
Iraq (Operation Iraqi Freedom, 2003–2010)

The attacks on the World Trade Center in New York and the Pentagon in Washington, D.C., on September 11, 2001, had forced the army into a transition—one akin to building an aircraft while flying. The impact of this transition was the creation of more brigade-level commands and more opportunities for African Americans to lead in combat. From the initial reports of the attacks, African-American brigadier generals Thomas Bostick and Montague Winfield were the Pentagon watch officers informing the president and the chairman of the joint chiefs of staff of the 9/11 events as they unfolded.

Legacy of African-American Military Leaders

As of this book's publishing, President Barack Obama is the commander-in-chief of U.S. military forces, and General William "Kip" Ward, commander, U.S. Africa Command (AFRICOM), is the only four-star general on active duty. All U.S. armed forces require troops and leaders to have a propensity to seek

Daniel James as a lieutenant general and vice commander of the Military Airlift Command in 1975. He would go on to become the first African-American to don four stars as commander-in-chief of the North American Air Defense Command. *U.S. Air Force*

Midshipman Wesley A. Brown, the first African-American to graduate from the U.S. Naval Academy, 1949. *U.S. Naval Historical Center*

Rear Admiral Samuel L. Gravely Jr., the first African American to hold flag rank in the U.S. Navy. *U.S. Naval Historical Center*

high-risk duty, but none more than the elite forces. (Historically, in the early years of America's elite forces, African Americans sought out elite assignments, especially at the enlisted levels.) To this point, there has still only been one African-American commander of an airborne division: Gen. Roscoe Robinson (now deceased). Within the special forces, there has been only one African-American special force general officer, Brig. Gen. Remo Butler, and only one known African-American officer within the action teams of the Delta Force.*

---

*Colonel Atkinson (ret): Officer's full name withheld.

Leading the Elite Forces

In 1976, Maj. Gen. Roscoe Robinson, who was promoted to brigadier general in only twenty years, became the first commanding general of the 82nd Airborne Division at Fort Bragg, North Carolina. He was also the first African-American four-star general.

The first African-American female general officer, Hazel Johnson, could attribute her success to army policy at the time she entered the U.S. Army—it was shortly after President Harry Truman banned segregation and discrimination in the armed services. In 1979, she became the first chief of the Army Nurse Corps.

General Colin Powell, Chairman of the Joint Chiefs of Staff, 1991. *Bachrach/Getty Images*

So What?

The U.S. Army, the most diverse and inclusive of all services—and indeed the military (the Department of Defense) as a whole—is losing African-American leaders. It has been the impetus for change in so many ways. The leaders of the 2030s and 2040s are in high school now, and if we don't renew our commitment, our willingness to shed our blood, we may not be able to enjoy its treasure as equal partners. The respect for military service still exists within the civilian community, but the collective desire to serve needs an overhaul, or there won't be more African-American four-star generals like those created from lieutenants

Sergeant Major Alford L. McMichael, USMC, was the fourteenth sergeant major of the United States Marine Corps (1999–2003), and was the first senior noncommissioned officer for Allied Command Operations for NATO (2003–2006). *USMC*

from the 1960s and 1970s—the only five black four-star generals in our history: Brig. Gen. Roscoe Robinson, Commander, Europe, and first African-American commander of the 82nd Airborne; Johnnie Wilson, Commander, Material Command—the nation's largest command; Larry Ellis, first African-American commander of Forces Command; or Kip Ward, Commander, AFRICOM, and the only African-American four-star general still on duty among all services.

Sergeant Major Carlton W. Kent, the current sergeant major of the Unites States Marine Corps, assuming the post on April 25, 2007. *USMC*

Rear Admiral Victor G. Guillory was selected to assume command of U.S. Naval Forces Southern Command/U.S. 4th Fleet in June 2009. *U.S. Navy*

John L. Estrada was the fifteenth Sergeant Major of the United States Marine Corps, succeeding Alford L. McMichael on June 26, 2003. Estrada stepped down on April 25, 2007. *USMC*

Enlisted leadership of platoon sergeants, first sergeants, and command sergeant majors remains disproportionately higher among African Americans than national representation and even within the army's enlisted ranks. The only serious study of this phenomenon, conducted in the mid-1990s, suggested that enlisted African Americans outperformed virtually every group of soldiers. Statistically, African Americans complete their first enlistment and stay in the military longer. Fourteen percent of those enrolled in the Reserve

Sergeant Andrew Dixon of the Pennsylvania Army National Guard's Marksmanship Training Unit demonstrates clearing procedures for the M240B machine gun during a weapons-familiarization class on May 14, 2010, at Fort Indiantown Gap, Pennsylvania. Dixon is a native of Lancaster, Pennsylvania. *U.S. Army*

Officer Training Corps (ROTC) African American; less than 10 percent of the cadets at West Point are African American. Arguably, it was Colin Powell's demonstrated military acumen and statesmanship, as the chairman of the Joint Chiefs of Staff, that convinced this nation an African American could be a great commander-in-chief.

Elite Units

The most elite of the army forces are the special operating forces, which include a myriad of selection techniques, intelligence collection, and training and direct-action forces. The army units in this category are Special Forces, Rangers, and Light Airborne forces. The most recognizable of these type forces are the U.S. Army Special Forces, or Green Berets, so named because of the unique, kelly green berets its members worn since the early 1960s. In the early 1970s, the U.S. Army formerly established ranger battalions, removing the ranger companies from division formations. These

Private First Class Matthew Starks, a petroleum-supply specialist assigned to Company G, 1st Battalion, 82nd Field Artillery Regiment, 3rd Brigade Combat Team, 82nd Airborne Division, only spent about a month in Iraq fueling vehicles. The Hayward, California, native is now a MRAP (mine-resistant, armor-protected) vehicle gunner. "As far back as I can remember, I always wanted to be a soldier," Starks said. *U.S. Army*

battalions were designed to be the premier light-infantry forces within the army, with the ability to carry out classified missions anywhere in the world.

During the 1980s, light divisions of 10,000 soldiers were created to augment the elite 82nd Airborne and 101st Airborne divisions—the only surviving airborne divisions of World War II.* These forces were augmentations to the mechanized and tank forces needed to combat Soviet forces. Additionally, they provided the army with the capability to address less-defined threats around the world. The primary focus of these forces was on jungle, mountainous, and urban environments; nations in Central and South America (in order to counter communist forces attempting to destabilize these areas with economic alliances and drugs); the Middle East; the Pacific Islands; and lastly, sub-Saharan Africa.

Lance Corporal William S. Gamble, a scout with Alpha Company, 2nd Light Armored Reconnaissance Battalion, conducts a personnel search at a vehicle checkpoint in the desert of Helmand province, Afghanistan, on May 16, 2010. The company's 2nd Platoon conducted 2,500 interdictions while maintaining the checkpoint. *U.S. Army*

---

*The 101st was converted to an air assault (helicopter) division in the late 1970s.

Conclusion

FROM OUR FIGHT for freedom, on both sides, during the Revolutionary War to today's Global War on Terror, African-American men and women have served their country with pride.

The Revolutionary War provided freedom for thousands of blacks in return for their service to the colonial army (and the British) and solidified the notion of freedom for countless others. Crispus Attucks and Salem Poor became legendary war heroes, the latter being granted his freedom directly from the U.S. Congress.

The Civil War fueled the rise of black political leaders like Frederick Douglass, who not only led the anti-slavery movement but personally recruited black troops to the Union war effort. Twenty-five black soldiers and seamen won the Medal of Honor, and the Confederacy was crushed with the help of black troops, ending slavery in this country forever.

Post–Civil War western expansion was accomplished with protection from the black 9th and 10th Cavalry "Buffalo Soldiers" and the 24th and 25th Infantry.

Although only one black soldier received the Medal of Honor during the First World War, the American Expeditionary Force's 93rd and 92nd divisions fought bravely and established a deadly combat reputation with their German enemies while gaining the nickname "Swartzentodt" or "Black Death." The 92nd boasted black junior officers trained at Fort Des Moines, Iowa, where black leadership was allowed at the division level for the first time.

World War II offered both the best and the worst of the black military experience: segregation made it a bitter memory for many black veterans, but black troops still made significant gains in combat. The 332nd Fighter Group "Tuskegee Airmen" secured the skies above North Africa and Europe while the 92nd Division and 758th Tank Battalion battled Nazi forces in Italy. The 761st Tank Battalion fought under legendary Gen. George Patton and liberated those held in Nazi death camps. Black Marines fought Imperial Japan in the South Pacific, where black Capt. James Morris broke the command color line with the 6th Army "Alamo Force." Black 92nd Division Lt. Vernon Baker won the Medal of Honor in Italy, although it was not awarded until half a century later, along with medals for six other black recipients. Some black women entered the military through the Women's Army Corps (WAC), and others served as nurses and factory workers, a few even typing up plans for the atomic bomb that ended the war. An even greater impact on black America was made by the post-war GI Bill that allowed thousands to attend college and become the black middle socioeconomic class of today.

Although President Truman's 1948 military desegregation order was largely ignored by the military establishment, the combat reality of a Chinese entrance into the Korean War made black troops a valuable commodity. Two soldiers of the 24th Infantry received the Medal of Honor for bravery in the Korean War, and black troops cemented the concept of racially integrated forces.

The Vietnam War provided additional combat opportunities that resulted in a 22 percent black casualty rate, especially after 1967 when black troop levels soared. Twenty black soldiers, marines, and seamen received the Medal of Honor for bravery in Vietnam, and a new class of black military leadership was born, led by Gen. Colin Powell.

Today's military continues to improve opportunities for black men and women, although societal racism remains an issue. The author of this book's foreword, retired Lt. Gen. Julius Becton Jr., co-chairs a Military Leadership Diversity Committee seeking command equality, while chapter 8 contributor Brig. Gen. Arnold Gordon-Bray represents a rising class of young black general officers.

As the challenges of the global war on terror become more complicated, our black male and female troops will continue to serve with pride and distinction and defend our nation. They always have, as you have read and seen in *Black Faces of War*.

I can credit this book to the appreciation of history instilled in me by my family at an early age. Be it military, civil rights, or literature, my love of history has led me down a path of awareness and provided knowledge of the many barriers broken down by brave black men and women against all odds. My grandparents, James and Georgine Morris Sr., and parents, James and Arlene Morris Jr., fed me a steady diet of history and reality from my childhood.

In addition to my grandfather's newspaper, I also thank Alex Haley's *Roots* for unlocking my quest for the truth about my family and my people from Virginia and Georgia through Maryland, Washington, D.C., and Iowa. The many black combat officers I have known through the years—including World War II veterans Virgil Dixon of the 758th Tankers, who is also my godfather, and Luther Smith and Joe Gomer, both Tuskegee Airmen—all boosted my interest. My recruitment of Gen. Colin Powell to my Fort Des Moines Memorial project in 1998 gave me the opportunity to gain a fresh perspective on today's military.

Despite the tremendous hardships they endured in the Jim Crow South, the bloody battlefields of Grandfather's World War I France, and the deadly islands of Dad's World War II South Pacific, never did any of my family express enduring hatred for white Americans or any other peacetime or wartime enemy. Surrounded by their combat veteran friends like World War I veteran Jimmy Mitchell, I heard first-person accounts from black officers who were there and lived to tell the story.

Obtaining education and gaining knowledge were always the goals of my family, from my great-grandmother Saleema, born into Georgia slavery in 1864, to all who have attended college and become leaders in their respected endeavors.

As for black military history, my combat officer grandfather and father provided a steady flow of education and contradictions of the many mistruths about black troops often spread by books, newspapers, and television. My civil rights leader grandmother and mother, who typed the final plans for the Atomic Bomb, played equally important roles in my development.

Growing up during the Vietnam War and throughout today's Global War on Terror, I have followed these great men and women as a free thinker and leader, which has benefited me in business and in creating unique military memorials at Fort Des Moines and IANG 132nd Fighter Wing, and now, this book.

Special thanks go to researcher Phil Parks and illustrators Amina Ali and Susan Koch Bridgeford for helping bring this project to life, and to my wife Vivian, daughter Jessica, and sons Robert and Brandon, who supported me throughout this historic project.

—Robert V. Morris

Works Cited

Chapter 1:

Botkin, B. A., ed. *A Treasury of Southern Folklore.* New York: Crown, 1949.

Brown, William Wells. *The Negro in the American Rebellion.* Boston: Lee & Shepard, 1867.

Franklin, John Hope. *From Slavery to Freedom: A History of Negro Americans.* New York, Knopf, 1967.

Hughes, Langston, and Arna Bontemps, eds. *The Book of Negro Folklore.* New York: Dodd, Mead, 1958.

Jordan, Winthrop D. *White Over Black.* Chapel Hill: University of North Carolina Press, 1968.

Katz, William L., ed. *Eyewitness: The Negro in American History.* New York, Pitman, 1967.

Lanning, Michael. *African Americans in the Revolutionary War.* New York: Kensington, 2000.

Stearns, George. *Narrative of Henry Box Brown.* Boston: Brown and Stearns, 1849.

Chapter 2:

Douglass, Frederick. *Selected Speeches and Writings.* Edited by Philip S. Foner. Chicago: Lawrence Hill, 1999.

National Archives: Adjutant General's Office, 1780–1917, Record Group 94.

Utley, Robert. *Frontier Regulars: The United States Army and the Indian, 1866–1890.* New York: Macmillan, 1973.

Chapter 3:

Archer-Straw, Petrine. *Negrophilia: Avant-Garde Paris and Black Culture in the 1920s.* London: Thames and Hudson, 2000.

Mitchell, James W. Interview by Elaine Estes and James Hatch, Des Moines, Iowa, February 20, 1975.

Morris, James B. Interview by Dr. Hal Chase, Des Moines, Iowa, November 4, 1974.

Morris, James B. Interview by Elaine Estes and James Hatch, Des Moines, Iowa, February 20, 1975.

Scott, Emmett J. *Scott's Official History of the American Negro in the World War.* Chicago: Homewood Press, 1919.

Thompson, John Lay. *History and Views of Colored Officers Training Camp.* Des Moines: *Iowa Bystander*, 1917.

Chapter 4:

Bellafaire, Judith A. *The Women's Army Corps: A Commemoration of World War II Service.* Washington, D.C.: Center of Military History, 1994.

Earley, Charity Adams. *One Woman's Army: A Black Officer Remembers the WAC.* College Station: Texas A&M University Press, 1989.

Roberts-Morris, Arlene. Interview by Robert Morris for Iowa Public Television, Johnston, Iowa, June 24, 1993.

Chapter 5:

Dixon, Vigil F. Interview by Robert V. Morris, July 1992.

Gomer, Joseph. Interview by Robert V. Morris, Des Moines, Iowa, November 3, 2009.

Oliphant, La Verna D. Address to the 13th Tuskegee Airmen National Convention, Sam Bruce Chapter, Atlanta, Georgia, 1984.

Smith, Luther H. Keynote speech at the Iowa Tuskegee Airmen Memorial Dinner, Marriott Hotel, Des Moines, Iowa, November 2, 2002.

Chapter 6:

Much of this chapter is drawn from James B. Morris Jr.'s military records and letters home from the South Pacific, 1942–1945 (Morris collection), and from research done in 1997 by Sterling H. Dover, Western Province Historian, Kappa Alpha Psi Fraternity, Seattle, Washington.

Chapter 7:

Becton, Julius W., Jr. *Becton: A Soldier and Public Servant.* Annapolis: Naval Institute Press, 2008.

Burnough, Clarence. Interview by Robert Morris for Iowa Public Television, Johnston, Iowa, August 11, 1992.

Harrell, Richard P. Interview by Robert V. Morris, Des Moines, Iowa, October 9, 2008.

Johnson, George W. Interview by Robert V. Morris, Omaha, Nebraska, October 7, 2008.

Index